AF255222

Serpent Crusher

Serpent Crusher

A Plan to Become a Better Man by
Crushing the Things That Crush You

Jeff Voth

WIPF & STOCK · Eugene, Oregon

SERPENT CRUSHER
A Plan to Become a Better Man by Crushing the Things That Crush You

Wipf & Stock
An Imprint of Wipf and Stock Publishers
199 W. 8th Ave., Suite 3
Eugene, OR 97401

www.wipfandstock.com

PAPERBACK ISBN: 978-1-6667-6310-2
HARDCOVER ISBN: 978-1-6667-6311-9
EBOOK ISBN: 978-1-6667-6312-6

05/23/23

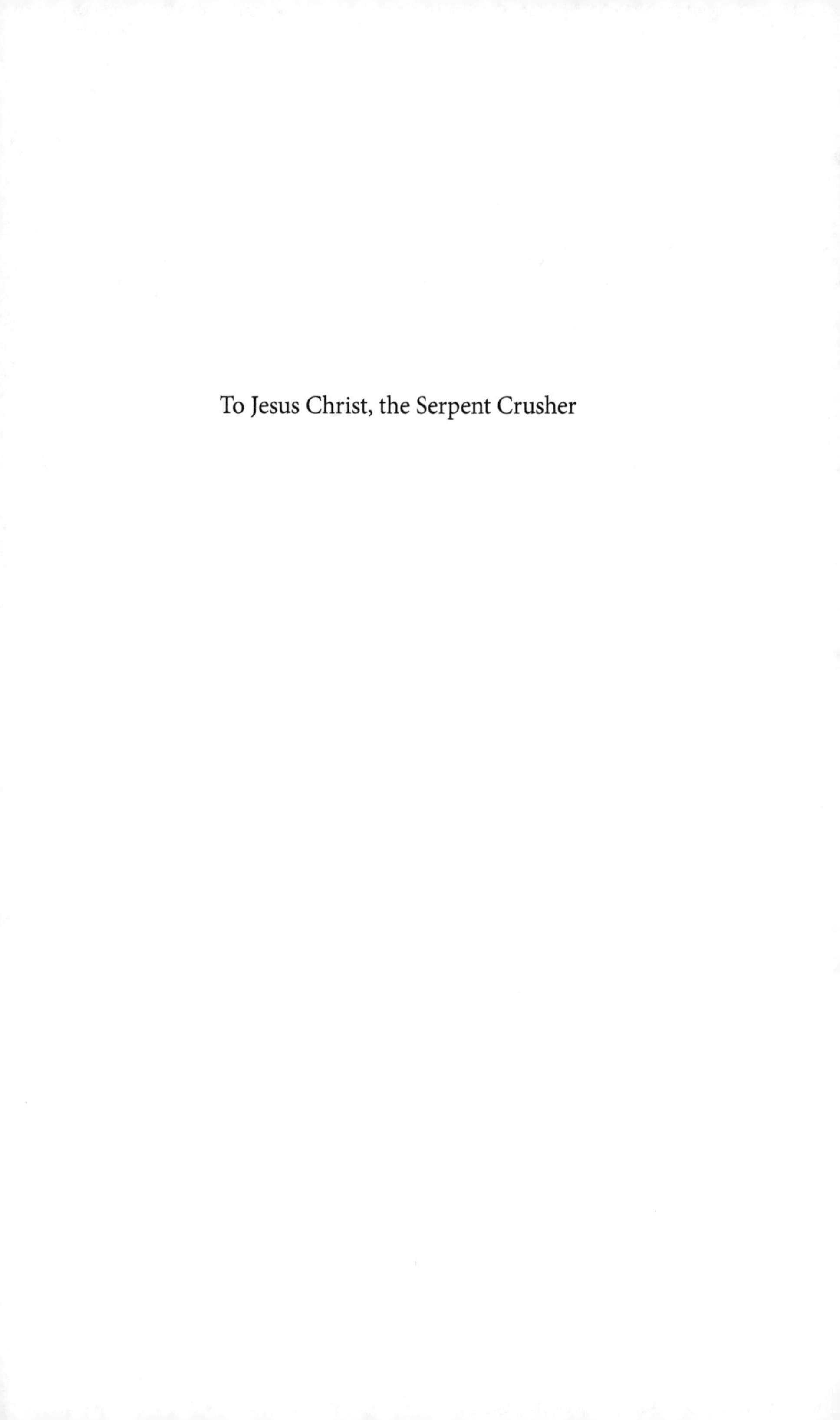

To Jesus Christ, the Serpent Crusher

Contents

Chapter 1: Getting Crushed | 1

Chapter 2: Becoming Crushers | 8

Chapter 3: Crushing Your Time | 23

Chapter 4: Crushing Your Health | 31

Chapter 5: Crushing Your Mouth | 42

Chapter 6: Crushing Your Mind | 50

Chapter 7: Crushing Your Sexuality | 59

Chapter 8: Crushing Your Heritage | 71

Chapter 9: Crushing Death | 81

Chapter 10: Serpent Crushing, Giant Slaying Rhythm | 88

Bibliography | 109

1

Getting Crushed

"Crush: to press something very hard so that it is broken or its shape is destroyed."—Cambridge Dictionary[1]

"What, ninety-one seconds?" I screamed. "How could someone get knocked out that quickly?" But it was true. On June 27, 1988, Mike Tyson knocked out heavyweight champion Michael Spinks in only ninety-one seconds. We were dirt poor campus missionaries and had no money at all. I had spent $60, which I didn't have, to record the fight live. We were attending a training seminar out of town. I was looking forward to coming home to watch an epic fifteen-round fight at a later date. What a waste. Spinks got crushed, and it was by a punch to the chest. Granted, it was Mike Tyson doing the punching, but it wasn't even a classic Tyson headshot. It was the weirdest crushing blow that I had ever seen.

While I had never experienced a crushing blow as Spinks had, I too would experience one that would send me to the canvas. I have always loved football. I was an okay little-leaguer but got hurt in high school. I became a wannabe college football player. I lived with a lot of "what ifs." What if I had played deeper into my high school years? What if I had gotten a shot? So, to answer all those questions and prove to myself and the world what a great

1. "Crush."

1

football player I could have been, I joined a team after college and played in several full-contact city flag football leagues. Some real football players have said that these leagues actually feel more dangerous than the ones in which they had played in college and the NFL even. This is due to the fact that there are no pads, in addition to the dangerous wannabes like me running all over the field and throwing their bodies around thoughtlessly.

As fate would have it, I was playing in an epic game one night. We were behind, and I was fired up to do something big. So, on the kick-off, I broke down to pull a guy's flag and make a touchdown-saving tackle. The last thing I remember about the breakdown was a flash of movement to my left. The flash was an opposing player I hadn't seen, zeroing in on my head. After that, everything turned to fog. When the fog cleared a couple of hours later, I found myself in a CT scan. With my wife Lori faithfully by my side in the emergency room, the doctors asked me questions I couldn't answer. I had gotten crushed—literally. My brain had gotten crushed and concussed. I am told that I actually popped up after the crushing blow and walked in circles a bit as I uttered foul language, ranting about the guy who had hit me. I had never been a cusser, so that tipped off my wife and the other guys on our church team that something was wrong. Yes, I failed to mention that this was a church team. Like Spinks ninety seconds into the Tyson fight, I too had been crushed.

Crushed Flat

If you haven't gotten the picture yet, let me give you one more visual of what getting crushed looks like. A couple of years ago, on the busy street where I drove to work, I noticed that the traffic in my lane had come to a virtual stop. Cars were creeping slowly by an object on the side of the road. Initially, I couldn't tell what it was, then something caught my eye. Due to the fact that I am a duck hunter, my eyes were drawn to a beautifully plumed Mallard drake. He was not flying like ones that usually catch my attention in the wild. This one was walking by himself in my lane. It was as if he owned the entire roadway. He didn't seem to be worried in the slightest about the vehicles that were crowding him either. In fact, when we got close to him, he didn't scurry. He actually looked back at me, quacked, and acted as if he were offended.

This scene repeated itself for a couple of weeks. I would see traffic slowing, then there he was again, walking in his lane. It was as if he were almost daring someone to mess with him. That was his road, and he would be damned if someone tried to convince him otherwise. Well, one day, he got convinced. I'm not sure who did it, nor exactly how it happened, but as I rolled up to the region on the asphalt where his usual morning parade took place, there he was. But this time, he wasn't strutting his glorious stuff. He was actually part of the asphalt. No blood, no splatter, no poof of feathers, he was flat, just like a piece of cardboard. In fact, that's what he looked like. He had been crushed and distorted into a figure that was not his natural shape.

Like Spinks, me as a wannabe footballer, and the flattened mallard, men are getting crushed. Through porn, sexual addiction, the objectification of all kinds of things, lethargy, and cluelessness regarding their purpose, men have lost their shape. They have been forced into a mold that was not initially intended for them, and they are totally out of whack. I have found that this is the case all over the world. In the last few years, I have had the chance to travel to Ireland, South Africa, Greece, and the US, and I am here to tell you that men are under assault. Every second there are 28,258 users watching pornography on the internet, spending a total of $3,075.64.[2] This is every second. Sadly, the main consumers are men.

The main consumers of sex-trafficked children are men.[3] There is undoubtedly an international assault on men. I have traveled to Ireland several times in the last few years and found the suicide rate for men especially alarming.[4] There are special patrols

2. "Internet Pornography by the Numbers," lines 30–33.

3. Williamson, Celia, "These are the Customers Who Support Sex-trafficking in the US," lines 20–21.

4. "National Office for Suicide Prevention Annual Report – 2021," 53.

assigned to bridges in an effort to prevent men from jumping off of them. In Greece, men are afraid they will not have work and a steady income. This is *not* what men were created for. They weren't created to be crushed by fear, lust, anger, depression, anxiety, and purposelessness. This isn't the shape that the creator intended for them. Why are men getting crushed?

Friends?

To answer the previous question, one needs to go all of the way back to the garden of Eden. Back to the point in the Genesis story when the man should have been at his most glorious and powerful place. There he was, in the garden, with his freshly formed, smoking hot wife, living the good life (see Gen 1–2). Then, somehow, he let his guard down. The serpent, who wasn't slithering on his belly yet, walked into his space and became Adam's friend. How else could he have gotten so welcomed into the lives of Adam and his wife Eve? So comfortable that he could invite and convince them to eat the forbidden fruit? (see Gen 3). I think he became such good friends with them that he convinced them to forget God's commands and get crushed into a shape that was not intended for them. A selfish, objectifying shape. How could he do this? Remi Adleke says that Satan has "immense intelligence" and that "if Satan can persuade a third of the angels in Heaven to rebel against God, how easy do you think it is for him to persuade us to believe that God doesn't exist?"[5] Essentially, if you think that you will outsmart the serpent, the slithering one, you are an idiot. You know the story. They get convinced to disobey then hide in their shame from the creator (see Gen 3:1–10). That is not the shape that they had originally been given. Not only did they hide in their shameful misshapenness; they started doing something that they had never done: playing the blame game. That wasn't their original shape, either. They were originally created to complement, support and "fit" one another—not blame and accuse. So, just like our original

5. Adeleke, "Every Hero Has A Villain."

parents in the garden, men and women have been disobeying, blaming, and arguing with each other since the dawn of time.

Get in Shape

Men need to get in shape. I'm not talking about getting a membership to 10Gym or the latest and greatest fitness gimmick, although doing a few sit-ups or jogging a half-mile wouldn't hurt any of us. I am talking about getting out of the shape many of us have been crushed into and into the manly, masculine shape for which we were created—a shape that is to bring the creator's dominion back to the planet. A crushed man can't do that. That's the purpose of this book: to get you out of your crushed shape and into the one for which God created you. We need to do better. We need to be better men. In fact, I have dedicated a fair amount of my adult life to helping men be better, to get out of their crushed state and into the one for which they were originally created. Cavetime is a ministry that I founded back in 2010, dedicated to helping men get better by practicing what we call the *five stones*: Show Up, Worship, Prayer, Word, and Community.[6] I have found that the application of these five habits, or disciplines, helps men become better: a better husband, a better father, a better man. Countless numbers of men have applied these disciplines and stopped getting crushed. But, I must admit, my audiences were mostly religious, and predominantly Christian, and while these guys needed to stop getting crushed and become better men, so do those who have no religious background. If we are totally transparent, we all need help to become better.

In the midst of this realization that all men needed much help, a passion was ignited inside of me, not just for the religious,

---

6. *Cavetime* by Jeff Voth is a book that identifies the ways the busyness of life can drain and distract men. These challenges can be countered by rediscovering one's refuge in God, and by engaging with the "stones," or disciplines, of showing up, worship, prayer, interacting with God's Word, and living in community. The Cavetime ministry exists to equip men in these areas through practical strategies and online tools.

Christian, church-going guy, but for all guys. I felt challenged by Jesus himself to come up with some non-religious language that would explain Cavetime to anyone. Language that was simple, clear, and focused—an elevator speech. So, I went to work. I have to admit that it wasn't easy either. I found myself often falling back into religious language and terminology that would undoubtedly alienate someone who didn't understand words like "ministry" or "spiritual." Then, after much toil, sweat, writing, erasing, and rewriting, I arrived at an explanation that took me literally ten seconds to say. Are you ready? Don't blink or you might miss it. "Cavetime is a company that I founded in 2010, dedicated to building better men." That's it. Short, concise, and easy to remember. In arriving at such a short explanation, my hope was that there would be a follow-up to the sixteen-word proclamation. Something like, "Better men? How do you do that? How do you make a better man?" To those questions, I would gladly offer, "Through extensive research, we have developed some habits and attitudes modeled after the lives of several very successful men, who have modeled their lives after the most successful man ever to walk the planet. By applying our discoveries, men will undoubtedly become better men." The next response would invariably have to be, "Who are these men?" or "Who is the most successful man to ever walk the planet?" I would then present them with our findings, which would ultimately draw them to Jesus, the best man ever. He is the superlative of masculinity. I wouldn't have to wait very long to see if my elevator speech was a good one.

The Elevator Speech

The airplane was packed full of people, and there was one seat left in the middle of my row. Maybe you've been there before? I was on the aisle and another man was next to the window. Tired and thankful that I could close my eyes, I settled in for my nap. However, just before the stewardess closed the hatch, a woman burst onto the plane. We were all awakened as she strolled down the aisle. She was physically fit and proud of it. In fact, with what she was wearing, she could have worked out on the plane. As fate would have it, or maybe as Jesus had planned it, she stopped at my row. "That's my seat. Want me to just step over you?" she said loudly. "No, that's okay", I said as I stepped out. She stowed her bag in the compartment above and plopped down into the seat in the middle, saying something under her breath. "So much for a nap," I thought to myself.

As she settled in, she became fixated on my shirt. Feeling a bit uncomfortable and unsure of what she was looking at, I glanced down. I forgot that I was wearing a shirt that said "Cavetime: South Africa" on the chest. As our eyes met, she inquired rather loudly, "Cavetime: South Africa, what's that?" Every nearby passenger who wasn't wearing their noise-canceling headphones (and some who were) were waiting for my response. What a great time for my newly crafted elevator speech. "Cavetime is a company that I founded in 2010, dedicated to building better men. We recently held a conference in South Africa." It rolled out easily and clearly. "I could use one of those. Where do I get one?" she retorted, immediately launching into a story about how she had been hurt by men and felt the need to be strong and handle things herself. I shared how we saw many men be turned into better men as they came to our events, read our materials and applied the practices to their lives. They were ultimately better because of Jesus, the best of men. The two hour flight felt like twenty minutes. My new friend had had an experience with a man who had been made better by Jesus. I am humbled that he has made me a better man and allows me to work with him to raise up as many better men as possible. Better men are an antidote to the message that men are toxic. Men acting like Jesus and his men are never toxic—they are an antidote for toxicity. They are a protective wall where people can hide, get safe, and become what they were intended to be. But, in order to do this, we are going to need to learn to *crush it* instead of being crushed.

2

Becoming Crushers

"Better: of a higher standard, or more suitable, pleasing, or effective than other things or people."—Cambridge Dictionary[1]

L ast chapter, we spoke about being better men and my elevator speech that I delivered to the woman on the airplane. I just want guys to know what being a better man feels like. When they feel it, it kind of grows on them. But so many guys have no idea what it feels like to be a better man. I remember the feeling back in junior high as I faced off with my opponent in the packed little gym. "Ready, wrestle!" yelled the ref. Then he blew his whistle and I shot across the little mat and grabbed my opponent in my patented Olympic headlock. Together we fell to the mat: me on top, him on the bottom. Eight seconds later, the ref slapped the mat and the epic battle was over—I had crushed that kid. Our team and fans leaped to their feet, and my hand was thrust into the air as the victor. I was a ninety-eight-pound crushing maniac. I felt like I was on top of the world. It also propelled me into a pretty decent junior high and senior high wrestling career as I figured I could crush anyone and anything that dared step on a mat with me. Now, that isn't exactly what happened every time, but I am telling you that

1. "Better."

I can still remember what the experience of being the crusher felt like, and I feel in some fashion that I am created to crush things.

That junior high experience ultimately set me up for the highlight of my high school wrestling career, too. Like it was yesterday, I remember our high school was wrestling our crosstown rivals in their gym. The gym was packed with hundreds of people. My parents were there. My youth pastor was there. My uncle, who had wrestled in college, was there. Lastly, but certainly not least, my girlfriend, the cheerleader, was there. The coach for the other team was a legend in the wrestling world, and my opponent was very formidable. It might have been daunting and intimidating for anyone else, but not for me that night. I knew what it was like to crush someone, and I wanted to crush it again. "Ready, wrestle." We locked up, I swung my hips with my back facing him and launched into, you guessed it, my patented Olympic headlock. I flung him in the air, and we landed just as I had landed many years before in junior high. He was on his back, the crowd went crazy, and all of my fans, family, and loved ones were smiling. I know so because someone snapped a pic and gave it to me a couple of years ago. Almost like it was yesterday, I was there. Seeing pictures of my elated fans and his dejected ones. I was crushing him, and he was getting crushed. I knew what it felt like and expected it to happen again.

Now, I would be a liar if I were to tell you that all of my matches happened like that, but quite a few did. I got used to winning and sometimes crushing my opponents. I contend that knowing what that felt like propelled me to do it again, or at least have the expectation that it would. These events can also happen in reverse. Men can expect to get crushed because that's what they have known. I am here to tell you that it doesn't have to be that way. Somehow you feel like a loser. Almost like you are cursed. I am here to tell you that you can reverse the curse. You just need to learn how to crush it instead of getting crushed. To do so, you need to look at some men who have crushed it throughout the years; then you will learn to do better, expect better, and be better. You will become a crusher. I have no doubt.

What Does "Better" and "Becoming a Crusher" Look Like?

So, what does a crusher look like? Well, it starts with a seed. A crusher's seed. For men who desire to follow the path God has for them, which is not to get crushed repeatedly, it starts in the garden of Eden. Remember that first epic wrestling match where man got crushed by the serpent, Satan. As we spoke about earlier, for some reason, he was lured into disobeying the creator and eating the forbidden fruit; and when he did, he was put into an Olympic headlock that was an eternal death grip. The narrative explains how Eve took some of the forbidden fruit and gave it to Adam, "who was with her" (Gen 3:1–7). He allowed her to be lied to and the creator to be disparaged. This set of tyrannical circumstances brought an eternal curse upon them and all of their descendants. A curse that has been deemed "the fall." Yes, a crushing, reverberating death knell to their relationship with the creator. His plans for an earthly kingdom were doomed. Their dominion was crushed. A death grip now holds every man, throwing him on his back the moment he enters this world.

The Lord himself was the official at the fall, and he started the match with a pronouncement to the competitors, Adam and Satan. To Satan, he announced:

> upon your belly you shall go, and dust you shall eat all the days of your life. I will put enmity between you and the woman, and between your offspring and hers; he will strike your head, and you will strike his heel. (Gen 3:14)

God had a plan—a plan that would be played out over the ensuing generations. A plan chronicled in the Bible that ultimately comes to fruition in the person of Jesus Christ. Yes, Jesus Christ was, in fact, God's plan in the garden—a prophetic hope on the darkest of all days. Theologians call it the "proto-evangelium," a term that actually means "first gospel." In the midst of the cataclysmic first fall, there was also a literal first seed of evangelistic hope—a seed that would travel miraculously through the generations.

The perfect seed of heaven would somehow be carried by specific, chosen, imperfect individuals; then, at the perfect time (Gal 4:4–7), the seed would be divinely brought to life by God's Spirit. Brought to life by faith and placed into a woman, growing as the God-Man, Jesus. He would be the one who would crush the head of the serpent. He would become the killer of death, dying sacrificially on behalf of fallen mankind (Rev 13:8). The God-Man, Jesus, would ultimately crush the one who had introduced disobedience, death, and all of their heinous byproducts into the garden. Genesis 3:14–15 recounts the events of that dark, prophetic, serpent-crushing day. The great English preacher Charles Simeon even called these verses "the sum and summary of the whole Bible."[2]

The Bible shows us how Jesus is the ultimate serpent crusher, but it is worthwhile to study the many other examples of serpent-crushing representatives in Scripture. We will focus only on a few, though each of these helps us understand Jesus in a greater light.

Serpent Crushing Highlights[3]

Theologian James Hamilton of the Harvard Divinity School states in his article, "The Skull Crushing Seed of the Woman," that:

> Bad guys get broken heads in the Bible. In some texts it is specifically stated that the ones shattered are serpents. The Serpent was told he would eat dust (Gen 3:14), and in several places the rebellious eat or lick dust. At points, a number of these images are used together, but the enmity between the seeds and some aspect of the curse are present in them all.[4]

With all due respect to Dr. Hamilton and a litany of other scholars who have written on this subject in compelling fashion, it doesn't take someone with a PhD to know that a serpent's head

2. Simeon, "Discourse 7."

3. Portions of this chapter are taken in part from *Jesus is the Thesis* by Jeff Voth and Joshua Beck, 59–68.

4. Hamilton, "Skull Crushing Seed," 34.

needs to be dealt with to finish the job entirely. It's in the head where the brain lives, thinking occurs, and strategies are planned. It is the head that needs to be smashed and pummeled into lifelessness. Whether that be through impaling, hanging, beheading, or crushing, everyone knows that, though crushing is often easier said than done. After Adam and Eve were kicked out of paradise, the seed of the serpent and the seed of the women immediately clashed. In the midst of sin and evil, God chose individuals to continue his plan and will, although even these "heroes" constantly struggled with their own serpents. However, there are many instances in which God used imperfect humans to crush some snakes. A few biblical examples of a serpent's head being crushed in some form or fashion in the Old Testament are as follows:

1. A woman named Jael (heroine) drives a peg through Sisera's (serpent seed) head (Judg 4; 5:26).

2. An unknown woman (heroine) throws a millstone from a wall onto Abimelech's (evil king, serpent seed) head (Judg 9:53).

3. Haman (serpent seed) is hanged by the neck on gallows he had prepared for Esther's (heroine) uncle (Esth 7).

4. Yahweh crushes the head "from the house of the wicked" (Hab 3:13 NIV).[5]

While there are many more examples that affirm God's continual reminding of his people and the serpent that he had not forgotten his prophecy in Gen 3:15, there is one reminder that stands out in grander fashion than all the others. This has to do mostly with the reputation and size of the serpent's seed carrier and the short-lived anonymity of the one carrying the kingdom seed of the woman.

5. Hamilton, "Skull Crushing Seed," 36.

A Giant Serpent

In 1 Sam 16 and 17, one of the most epic serpent-crushing tales in all of literature exists: the battle between David and Goliath. The unknown shepherd David, son of Jesse, is identified by God to Samuel, the prophet/judge and anointed king. He would be identified for his God-focused "heart" and not necessarily his physical appearance. At his intimate anointing ceremony before his family and God, the narrative informs the reader that the Spirit, ". . . came upon David in power" (1 Sam 16:13). God had noticed and chosen the young man David, just like he had done in the case of the other seed carriers. Although he was anonymous to others and not even revered in his own household, he had been singled out by God to carry the kingdom seed. In fact, his name is listed in both lineages of the ultimate serpent crusher, Jesus (Matt 1:1; 1:6, Luke 3:31). King David would be used to carry the seed and perpetuate it to Jesus. Jesus would be called the "Son of David" on several occasions (Matt 1:1; Mark 12:35–37; Luke 1:32). This sonship would rightfully place him on the throne of David as the eternal heir to the promise of God to David in 2 Sam 7:16: "Your house and your kingdom shall be made sure forever before me; your throne shall be established forever." Therefore, Jesus Christ would be known as the Son of David and would rightfully inherit David's throne. The kingdom seed of the woman, the eternal serpent crusher, would be an eternal king. As the anointed king of his nation and carrier of the serpent-crushing seed, God intended to use this young man in extraordinary fashion and thereby make an extraordinarily loud and large statement to all the world.

The stage for this historic battle was the Valley of Elah, only fifteen miles west of David's hometown of Bethlehem and twelve miles from Hebron, the young nation's first home base. It was essentially right down the street in military terms. For some undisclosed reason, the leaders had chosen the type of conflict that called for two champions to meet in front of their respective armies and fight to the death. The winner then took all the spoils. And by all the spoils, it was known that family, livestock, land and everything else that a man owned would become property of the victor. Hope was nowhere to be found. This was due greatly to the fact that King Saul, the supposed champion of God's army, was hiding in his tent while a Philistine giant named Goliath appeared daily, heaving vile curses and threats at them.

What seemed to be a certain defeat hung over the battlefield like a thick fog. There was neither a plan nor a ray of hope. The serpent's seed had certainly slithered into the dominant position. Kingdom seed was once again on the brink of extinction. However, with God and the perpetuation of his seed, hope is eternal and, as has been seen in this age-old, enmity-filled conflict, it often shines in unlikely places and through unassuming, faith-filled faces. On that day in the Valley of Elah, the face belonged to a ruddy teenager who had been sent from Bethlehem by his father to bring food to his brothers who were on the battle lines hiding in intimidation. A faith-filled face that would beam brightly from the light of a fire-kindled heart—a fire that would not be doused by intimidating words or actions.

The intimidating words were ultimately hurled directly at David as he bravely volunteered to confront the giant, then calmly stepped onto the battlefield with his pouch, five smooth stones, sling and staff:

> 43 He said to David, "Am I a dog, that you come to me with sticks?" And the Philistine cursed David by his gods. 44 The Philistine said to David, "Come to me, and I will give your flesh to the birds of the air and to the wild animals of the field." (1 Sam 17:43)

The seed of the serpent and the kingdom seed of the woman face to face in a duel with ancient implements of war and eternal implications. Huge spears, slings, stones, javelins, and swords were at their ready. The carrier of the kingdom seed responded with steely courage, tethered to the name and reputation of his God, the God whom he knew personally and who had uttered the proto-evangelium himself thousands of years before:

> 45 But David said to the Philistine, "You come to me
> with sword and spear and javelin; but I come to you in
> the name of the Lord of hosts, the God of the armies of
> Israel, whom you have defied. 46 This very day the Lord
> will deliver you into my hand, and I will strike you down
> and cut off your head; and I will give the dead bodies of
> the Philistine army this very day to the birds of the air
> and to the wild animals of the earth, so that all the earth
> may know that there is a God in Israel, 47 and that all this
> assembly may know that the Lord does not save by sword
> and spear; for the battle is the Lord's and he will give you
> into our hand." (1 Sam 17:45–47)

Like a flash of lightning, and as he had certainly done thousands of times before while tending his father's sheep, David reached into his pouch, loaded a stone, then slung it from his sling towards the huge target lumbering towards him. The crush was quick and deep, followed by an earth-shaking thud. A cloud of dust rose as the onlookers stared in disbelief. The narrative recounts those epic moments:

> David ran quickly toward the battle line to meet the Philistine. 49 David put his hand in his bag, took out a stone, slung it, and struck the Philistine on his forehead; the stone sank into his forehead, and he fell face down on the ground. 50 So David prevailed over the Philistine with a sling and a stone, striking down the Philistine and killing him; there was no sword in David's hand. 51 Then David ran and stood over the Philistine; he grasped his sword, drew it out of its sheath, and killed him; then he cut off his head with it. (1 Sam 17:48b–51)

In a few short seconds, the tide had turned. Hope now shone brightly through the settling dust of Elah's battlefield. The serpent seed's head had been stealthily crushed, then decapitated for all the world to see. There was a new champion. One who, with a bloody trophy in his hands, would scream loudly that there was a God in his nation. David would harken back to that glorious day often in his psalms:

> But God will shatter the heads of his enemies, the hairy crown of those who walk in their guilty ways. (Ps 68:21)

> 12 Yet God my King is from of old, working salvation in the earth. 13 You divided the sea by your might; you broke the heads of the dragons in the waters. 14 You crushed the heads of Leviathan; you gave him as food for the creatures of the wilderness. (Ps 74:12–14)

David himself would keep Goliath's broken head, following a gruesome custom of the day. I have always wondered where this gargantuan trophy ended up, which led me to some deeper research. One scholar, Dr. Taylor Marshall, believes that the giant's head was ultimately kept in a famously infamous place:

> This would explain why the "place of the skull" is oddly named "Golgotha." The term is a corruption of Hebrew for "Goliath Gath": Goliath Gath > GoliGath > GolGath > GolGatha. So King David killed the enemy of Israel (Goliath of Gath) and then brought the giant's head to Jerusalem. Jews would not have permitted the Gentile giant's head to be buried in the city walls. It would have been buried outside the city walls. This matches with what we know about the location of Golgatha. It was outside the city walls. The slaying of Goliath by David was one of the most important events in "Israelite history." The location of the giant's head would have been known by all. Hence, "Golgatha" is likely the the place of not just any old skull, but the place of the skull of Goliath of Gath.[6]

Professor Rick Shenk agrees with Marshall and gives context to the magnitude of the battle between David and Goliath and its accompanying ramifications:

> This battle was not merely about Philistines and Israelites; it was about who rules over heaven and earth: the Serpent or YHWH! And now comes David, not with Serpent armor or weapons, but with powerful declarations: "this day YHWH will deliver you into my hand, and I will strike you down and cut off your head" (1 Samuel

6. Marshall, "Golgotha."

17:46). That should ring a bell for us! Indeed, David proceeds to bruise Goliath on the head with a stone. The Serpent–warrior fell on his face and ate dust. And then, David removed Goliath's head with his enemy's own sword. In this battle against the Serpent, the seed won! . . .Whether or not Goliath of Gath is the correct etymology of Golgotha, it was in this very city to which the head of Goliath was taken. It was on this very hill where Jesus' feet were pierced by the nails. It was in this very place that he crushed the head of the Serpent.[7]

"It is Finished"

It would be another one thousand years until Jesus, the Son of David, would triumphantly utter the words "it is finished" on Golgotha, the place of the skull (John 19:30). But, during that time, the seed would pass from David through the generations, ultimately being brought to life at the perfect time. The apostle Paul describes the miraculous occurrence: "But when the fullness of time had come, God sent his Son, born of a woman . . ." (Gal 4:4).

That's why it is so important to read the lineage of Jesus in the Gospels. They are the record of the kingdom seed of the woman, traveling miraculously through time. God used imperfect, faith-filled people throughout the ages to accomplish his perfect redemptive plan. The plan that he had prophesied in the garden in Gen 3:14–15. It had come to its full fruition in Jesus. Let's read the list of names. Some will be recognizable and some will not. Some pronounceable and some not. But all of them, set in place and in line, perfectly released in full force the serpent-crushing seed to accomplish his eternal work . . .

> *Jesus was about thirty years old when he began his work.*
> *he was the son (as was thought) of Joseph*
> *son of Heli, son of Matthat,*
> *son of Levi, son of Melchi,*

7. Shenk, "David and Goliath."

son of Jannai, son of Joseph,
son of Mattathias, son of Amos,
son of Nahum, son of Esli,
son of Naggai, son of Maath,
son of Mattathias, son of Semein,
son of Josech, son of Joda,
son of Joanan, son of Rhesa,
son of Zerubbabel, son of Shealtiel,
son of Neri, son of Melchi,
son of Addi, son of Cosam,
son of Elmadam, son of Er,
son of Joshua, son of Eliezer,
son of Jorim, son of Matthat,
son of Levi, son of Simeon,
son of Judah, son of Joseph,
son of Jonam, son of Eliakim,
son of Melea, son of Menna,
son of Mattatha, son of Nathan,
son of David, son of Jesse,
son of Obed, son of Boaz,
son of Sala, son of Nahshon,
son of Amminadab, son of Admin,
son of Arni, son of Hezron, son of Perez,
son of Judah, son of Jacob,
son of Isaac, son of Abraham,
son of Terah, son of Nahor,
son of Serug, son of Reu,
son of Peleg, son of Eber,
son of Shelah, son of Cainan,
son of Arphaxad, son of Shem,
son of Noah, son of Lamech,
son of Methuselah, son of Enoch,
son of Jared, son of Mahalaleel,
son of Cainan, son of Enos,

son of Seth, son of Adam,
the son of God.

Luke 3:23–38

The Second Adam

In the perfect timing of God, the seed had been carried through time by the aforementioned individuals. God had used them, through faith, to birth an entirely new race of humanity—a second Adam. An Adam who would not fail. One who would not fall. He would travel through broken humanity, live on a broken planet, then be impaled on a cross to bleed for the broken. The serpent would strike at his heel, bloodying him. Then, after bleeding on that skull of a rock called Golgotha, for all the world to see, he would declare, "It is finished." A crushing and eternal blow delivered to the serpent's head. The first Adam's penalty, which overshadowed all his children, was paid for by the untainted blood of the second. Then, an unexpected (for the serpent) second blow: an eternal nail to death. The crushed serpent, now forever beheaded. Jesus was alive. He had risen from the dead according to the Scriptures. Never before was there one like him, nor will there ever be again. He is the first and last of his kind. He is solely unique and uniquely sole. He is the "Alpha and the Omega" (Rev 1:8; 22:31). For those who will follow him, by faith, there lives an eternal hope, that they too, through him in them, will live by his life. It will be a new life where *all* things will be ". . . made new" (2 Cor 5:17). They too will crush the serpent all day long and for eternity.

We, as those who follow him, are called to live and establish serpent crushing communities all over the world. Communities where the alive, resurrected, serpent-crushing Jesus is the center . . . he is the thesis. Where individuals set about following a living, serpent-crushing savior. One who eats with them, teaches them, gives them marching orders, then empowers them to march. Luke, in the book of Acts, recounts what Jesus instructing and empowering the first communities looked like:

3 After his suffering, he presented himself to them and gave many convincing proofs that he was alive. He appeared to them over a period of forty days and spoke about the kingdom of God. 4 On one occasion, while he was eating with them, he gave them this command: "Do not leave Jerusalem, but wait for the gift my Father promised, which you have heard me speak about. 5 For John baptized with water, but in a few days you will be baptized with the Holy Spirit." 6 Then they gathered around him and asked him, "Lord, are you at this time going to restore the kingdom to Israel?" 7 He said to them: "It is not for you to know the times or dates the Father has set by his own authority. 8 But you will receive power when the Holy Spirit comes on you; and you will be my witnesses in Jerusalem, and in all Judea and Samaria, and to the ends of the earth." (Acts 1:3-8)

Jesus has already won the victory through his death and resurrection, and he will one day pin his opponent flat to the mat. Evil will be conquered for eternity on that last day. But until he does, this battle must be waged through people who call on his name. So, in the following chapters, we will establish what a serpent-crushing rhythm looks like. We will answer the questions: What does a serpent crusher think? How does a serpent crusher act? How does a serpent crusher train? It is our goal to develop serpent-crushing tactics highlighted throughout the Bible and ultimately lived out fully and perfectly in the greatest of *all* serpent crushers . . . Jesus Christ.

How To CRUSH IT

Every chapter will end by analyzing the different areas in which serpent crushers engage. This section will specifically address each chapter's focus. These steps teach a man how to *crush it*:

C–Call on the Name of the Lord

Calling is an intentional action. This first step represents the initial choice to look towards heaven in the midst of a challenge. It is the pause, the deep breath, the inward and skyward look into Christ's eyes. This reset is needed to realign one's focus with his.

R–Recall What He Has Done for You

Remind yourself of God's faithfulness and character. Reflect on both universal truths, such as the cross, empty grave, and/or personal truths; such as the ways God has healed you. Look past temporary distractions and cling to the truth.

U–Unleash the Authority of Heaven against the Serpent

Utilizing God's Word, speak a prayer against the challenge or situation you face. Command it to submit to Christ, who is over all things. Commit this challenge to regular, rhythmic prayer.

S–Stand

Continue your prayer by incorporating God's truth into your habits and lifestyle. Beyond words, allow Christ's power to inform your actions throughout your daily life.

H–Hold the Line

Invite other believers to join you in your pursuit of Christ. Struggle well in the context of community. Never isolate yourself from God's people.

IT–Whatever Serpent is Stalking You

The serpent is the deceiver, the one who tempts us to compromise our beliefs and seek fulfillment and value in sources other than God. Sources other than God, can become serpents in and of themselves. These areas are the ones to be crushed by the serpent crusher as he lives in and through us.

3

Crushing Your Time

"How can I lead people into the quiet place beside the still waters if I am in perpetual motion? How can I persuade a person to live by faith and not by works if I have to juggle my schedule constantly to make everything fit into place?"—Eugene Peterson, *The Contemplative Pastor*[1]

"We need to remember that our strength lies not in hurried efforts and ceaseless long hours, but in our quietness and confidence. The world today says, 'Enough is not enough.' Christ answers softly, 'Enough is enough.'"
—Tim Hansel, *When I Relax I Feel Guilty*[2]

Relationships and Regret

In the 2005 film rendition of *The Lion, the Witch, and the Wardrobe*, Lucy, one of the main characters, finds her friend Tumnus has been turned to stone by the evil witch. Upon seeing Tumnus, Lucy breaks into tears. She simply wanted more time with her friend, and it seemed that only tragedy remained where there once was a relationship. Although Tumnus would be brought back to life by Aslan, many of us are familiar with the emotions Lucy

1. Peterson, *Contemplative Pastor*, 19.
2. Hansel, *When I Relax I Feel Guilty*, 55.

experienced.[3] I have been a pastor for almost four decades and have done more funerals than I can count. I can't remember one person who has told me that they wish they had had more time to make money, more time to be busy, more time to be totally worn out, or more time for whatever else you can think of to fill in the blank. But I have had many tell me that they wished they had told someone that they had loved them just one more time or had been able to spend a little more time with them. Relationships: the ultimate purpose for which we have been placed on this planet. I am proposing that you budget your time to allow for them. No, let me correct that. Not to just allow for them, but to plan around them. To prioritize them. To be about healthy, happy, productive, fun, joyous, and mutually beneficial relationships. The creator did not give us life in order to spend it on that which will not last: money, houses, boats, stuff, and more stuff. Stuff that will rot, corrode, and waste away. It was Thoreau who said that the mass of men "live lives of quiet desperation."[4] That is why another old sage once said to me that "the richest square mile on earth was the graveyard." So many dreams, visions, and potential for lasting, loving relationships are buried there. So many live and die—but for what?

Go Where the Money Is

"I really wanted to be a coach. I loved coaching and working with athletes. It made me come alive. Especially when I would see them come alive. But I chose the field I am in now because my dad told me to go where the money was. I did that and I hate it. I get sick when I think about going to work tomorrow. I'm depressed. My wife is mad that I'm depressed and I'm too old to start over." I pleaded with the guy who said these things to me to consider a career restart. I challenged him to get some schooling, take a job on the side, and to do something to invest his life into the thing that

3. Adamson, *Chronicles of Narnia*. This scene was depicted in more detail in the film than in Lewis' book. The book does not describe Lucy's emotions upon seeing her friend turned to stone as the film portrayed.

4. Thoreau, *Walden*, 6.

made him come alive and then share it with others. Make it about relationships, not the money. The other stuff will take care of itself if you are coming alive every day, and, while no job is perfect, why not love what you do with your life and, at the same time, get paid for it? If that is the case, then it's not work, is it?

Old Testament: Moses and Delegation

Moses had a career reset at eighty-four. Can you imagine that? Hearing from God after your family had been raised and you had had a successful career in the most powerful government in the world? That was what happened to Moses. You can read the first part of the story in Exod 2. You will see that he was a celebrated governmental official who had been hand-picked by God for a special position—then it all blew up. He took a stand to bring about justice for his people and no one stood with him—so, he ran. He ran and he ran and he ran—to the back side of the desert. Then he hid there. But it is impossible to hide from the omnipotent God who made him and called him in the first place. He was found, and in an amazing interaction with God in the form of a burning bush (Exod 3), Moses had a career reset. He was called to go to Pharaoh, on behalf of the God who found him. God told him to "let my (God's) people go." Moses was thrust into a very intimate relationship with God. They would talk and walk and have agreements and disagreements. God would use him to set millions and millions of people free. But with people come relationships, and with relationships comes time. Who do I spend time with, and for how long?

For Moses, the task was insurmountable. Think about it. If there were only one million people, and that equaled one million families, and you spent 10–15 minutes listening to the problems of each family, how many minutes is that? How could you ever give them any quality time? So, Moses was actually functioning in the job God had for him, but he was still getting crushed. In fact, it is said that he would spend literally all of his waking hours listening to the people share their problems with him. He was being eaten alive by his job. Have you ever felt like this? If so, your time is getting crushed. Your life is being spent totally on the task and not serving the God who called you to the task. The serpent is coiling around you like a python, and you can't breathe. You know what? What you're doing is not wise.

"What You Are Doing is Not Good"

These were the words of Moses' father-in-law Jethro. In fact, here is his speech:

> 17 "What you are doing is not good. 18 You will surely wear yourself out, both you and these people with you. For the task is too heavy for you; you cannot do it alone. 19 Now listen to me. I will give you counsel, and God be with you! You should represent the people before God, and you should bring their cases before God; 20 teach them the statutes and instructions and make known to them the way they are to go and the things they are to do. 21 You should also look for able men among all the people, men who fear God, are trustworthy, and hate dishonest gain; set such men over them as officers over thousands, hundreds, fifties and tens. 22 Let them sit as judges for the people at all times; let them bring every important case to you, but decide every minor case themselves. So it will be easier for you, and they will bear the burden with you. 23 If you do this, and God so commands you, then you will be able to endure, and all these people will go to their home in peace." (Exod 18:17–23)

Moses heeded God's advice to him through the old sage, and he started doing things differently. He poured himself into some men, who poured themselves into some men and so on and so forth until all of the people were cared for. This is how God cares for his people. He is about relationships and time being poured into one another through that vehicle. Whether you are a business professional, minister, policeman, lawyer, trash collector, or the president of a nation, God wants to use you to establish relationships so that he might relate to people through you. He will use your gifts and talents to reach and relate to people and build his Kingdom. Moses ultimately got it too. Many people don't know it, but he actually wrote one of the psalms. Psalm 90 speaks of his relationship with his God and how God taught him how to number his days; that is, to establish a timely rhythm that isn't about just making money, acquiring power, or gaining fame. And while Moses accomplished some amazing things, making some in the midst of his battle with the serpent, he accomplished his purpose to take the cause of the serpent crusher to the next generation.

Jesus Crushed His Time

Do you think Jesus might have been busy? I do too. Quite a job it was, saving the world. There were places to go, people to save, demons to cast out, people to heal, dead friends to be raised. He ran hard for three and a half years—then he had the audacity to say "it is finished." Finished? How could that be? When he died, weren't there still people going to hell? Weren't there still demons running free? Weren't governments being used by darkness and evil? How, then, could Jesus say those words, "it is finished"? Maybe, just maybe, he did exactly what he had come to do. Could it be that he had done his job, and it was now someone else's job to finish? he had and continues to crush the giant that comes and tries to crush our time. So how did he crush the giant of time?

Charles Hummel suggests, "What was the secret of Jesus' ministry? We discover a clue in Mark's report of what happened after the very busy day of teaching and healing which we first noted. 'Very early in the morning, while it was still dark, Jesus got up, left the house and went off to a solitary place, where he prayed' (Mark 1:35). *He prayerfully waited for his Father's instructions.*"[5]

First, he spent much time with the Father, getting advice, insight, and time with the infinite one. He understood that as a man, he needed to have the insight of the one who was outside of time. The one who was not bound by a space-time continuum. The one who could see everything at the same time was speaking to his

5. Hummel, *Tyranny of the Urgent*, 9.

son about where he was to go, what he was to do, and for how long he was to do it, with the ultimate goal being the crucifixion. Jesus had to be about getting to the cross and getting the job done . . . finished. Second, he went away from crowds and the pull of culture to care about likes on social media and popular applause. This was not his motivation. That's why Peter could come to him and say, "Everyone is searching for you," and Jesus would say, "Let us go on to the neighboring towns, so that I may proclaim the message there also; for that is what I came to do" (Mark 1:37–38). He had come to go to specific places at specific times, to meet with specific people, then finish at the cross. Third, you could say that he had a rhythm—a rhythm that was dictated by his Father and not driven by crowds and the perceived needs of the people. Perceived needs of the people are not always the most important needs of the people. People often feel that their appetites and preferences dictate their needs, and then they want you to satiate those desires. The only fulfilling force in the lives of the people will be God through the person of Jesus, and Jesus had a rhythm that was empowered by that fact. He would not be deterred from this rhythm either. When Peter, one of his inner circle, rebuked him for saying he would have to be killed, Jesus turned and responded, "Get behind me, Satan!" (Matt 16:21–23). Jesus would crush the serpent who tried to *crush* his time.

CRUSH IT

C–Call on the Name of the Lord

Take a breath. Regularly pause at the beginning of your day (and in the middle of it) to turn your eyes towards Jesus. Look beyond the immediate concerns and responsibilities, towards Christ, breathing deeply as you pause in his presence.

R–Recall What He Has Done for You

Remind yourself of all of the hectic seasons that God has walked with you through, especially if you feel overwhelmed by the responsibilities of the day. Look at the big picture of God's continuing, eternal faithfulness.

U–Unleash the Authority of Heaven against the Serpent

Turn these first two steps into a prayer. Speak against the spirit of hurry and urgency. Speak with God slowly, and surrender your schedule and thoughts to him. Meditate and repeat a scripture that teaches this. Psalm 63 is one example of a passage that you might use to unleash the authority of heaven against the serpents trying to entangle you:

> *1 O God, you are my God, I seek you,*
> *my soul thirsts for you;*
> *my flesh faints for you,*
> *as in a dry and weary land where there is no water.*
> *2 So I have looked upon you in the sanctuary,*
> *beholding your power and glory.*
> *3 Because your steadfast love is better than life,*
> *my lips will praise you.*
> *4 So I will bless you as long as I live;*
> *I will lift up my hands and call on your name.*
> *5 My soul is satisfied as with a rich feast,*
> *and my mouth praises you with joyful lips*
> *6 when I think of you on my bed,*
> *and meditate on you in the watches of the night;*
> *7 for you have been my help,*
> *and in the shadow of your wings I sing for joy.*
> *8 My soul clings to you;*
> *your right hand upholds me.*
> *9 But those who seek to destroy my life*

shall go down into the depths of the earth;
10 they shall be given over to the power of the sword,
they shall be prey for jackals.
11 But the king shall rejoice in God;
all who swear by him shall exult,
for the mouths of liars will be stopped.

S–Stand

Choose your schedule, don't allow it to choose you. Incorporate a planner or calendar into your normal rhythm, designating specific times for Jesus, work, family, physical activity, and relaxation. Do this prayerfully so that your schedule reflects the priorities of your serpent-crushing king.

H–Hold the Line

In your schedule, try to plan at least one time a week to meet or talk with another believer. Prioritize godly community in your schedule, and speak with others about how to be successful in this area. Find someone that you see doing this well and ask to meet with them for the purpose of discussing how they hold the line in regards to their time.

IT–Your Time

The serpent would like to crush you with laziness, or by getting you so busy that you burn out. Jesus leads us into rest and purpose. In him, we can be effective for the kingdom community, while at the same time he leads us individually.

4

Crushing Your Health

"It is not the mountain we conquer but ourselves."
—Sir Edmund Hillary[1]

While Hillary was speaking in the quote above about climbing Everest, the simple truth in those nine words is deep—or should I say, high? Or both deep and high? That's because it can really be applied to all areas of life and existence, not just mountain climbing. There are actually many aspects of our existence that might not be as obviously intimidating or difficult to climb as a 29,032-foot-high mountain peak but for some people may be every bit as daunting. How about weight loss? Heart health? Cardiovascular health? General fitness level? Am I stepping on your toes yet? I hope so. It's good for all of us. Maybe I'm just being extra sensitive because I got mine stepped on recently. They are still stinging too. The stepping was done by my doctor, whom I thought was a friend. I hadn't seen him in a few years because of the potential for this type of embarrassing and maddening interaction. I hate visits to the doctor. I don't like getting my toes stepped on, and/or my sensitive ego crushed.

"You are technically obese. Decrease your sugar intake and lose 15 pounds," said the guy whom I thought was my friend. Ouch, I thought—that hurt. Hurt the ego housed inside of the

1. Steigerwald, "Lofty Ideals."

body that had just been labeled as obese. Racing through my head were all sorts of excuses. Excuses like, "I'm thick-boned," "muscularly dense," or "husky." While some of those might have been kind of true, the bottom line was that there were some aspects of my health that weren't so healthy. After the initial embarrassment and shock had worn off a bit, I started to process what the doctor was telling me. I needed to pay attention to some habits in my life that weren't so healthy. Habits that had begun to affect my blood sugar levels, my heart health, and my overall body composition. And if I didn't pay attention to those things, there could be some serious health ramifications. Ultimately, these ramifications could greatly impede my ability to live a vibrant life and do the things that God had put me on the earth to do. In fact, if I didn't pay attention to these issues, I could die. Ouch.

Two Sides of the Same Coin

There are those who would say that it's the spiritual things that are most important. Often, they do so with cream from the donut they just ate on their lips, or grease from that deep-fat-fried morsel of something. Sadly, many of these folks can spout huge portions of Scripture but couldn't walk a single flight of stairs without hyperventilating. This is a shame—a shame because our physical existence is deeply and mysteriously tied to our spiritual one. Humanity is the only creation into which God breathed his life. Since we exist as spiritual and physical creatures, spiritual and physical health directly affect one another; they are inextricably intertwined. The states of our existence are two sides of the same coin, distinct yet one. If one side gets bent out of shape, the other is sure to follow.

Spiritual and physical realities are interwoven throughout our various appetites and desires, as well as in our ability (or inability) to engage in the physical aspects of life. Our inability to make our physicality obey us, rather than the other way around, is a non-physical challenge just as much as it is a physical one. This chapter will primarily speak to physical health, whereas chapter six, "What Crushing Your Mind Looks Like," will explore mental and emotional health.

Bree the horse, a fictitious character in C. S. Lewis' *The Horse and His Boy*, experienced the negative effects of slavery that lasted beyond his physical enslavement. In the story, the narrator comments:

> "But one of the worst results of being a slave and being forced to do things is that when there is no one to force you any more you find you have almost lost the power of forcing yourself."[2]

The enduring bondage of enslavement can be an oppressive weight even after the shackles are gone. Even when the slave master isn't physically present, slavery is. It's a mindset. An all-encompassing way of existing—or non-existing. Being present but having lost the ability to resist or change. While the comment wasn't necessarily pertaining to physical health per se, it is still quite applicable; especially in regards to the intertwined nature of unhealthy physical, mental, and spiritual habits, and the fact that they collectively impact one another.

Habits and Discipline

Journalist Charles Duhigg has done substantial work in the areas of forming and changing habits and has found that . . .

> Most of the choices we make each day may feel like the products of well-considered decision-making, but they're not. They're habits. And though each habit means relatively little on its own, over time, the meals we order, what we say to our kids each night, whether we save or spend, how often we exercise, and the way we organize our thoughts and work routines have enormous impacts on our health, productivity, financial security, and happiness.[3]

---

2. Lewis, *Horse and His Boy*, 146.

3. Duhigg, *Power of Habit*, xvi.

The fact of the matter is that many Americans are physically sick in some form or fashion and often these illnesses are avoidable. Many are obese and/or severely obese.[4] According to my physician, I am one of them. It hurts to even write that. But maybe it needs to hurt—hurt so much that I start to crush it with some new physical habits. Said like a true American. In 2020, we spent $828 billion on physical activity products and services, leading the world in this category, yet placed twentieth on the international stage in participation in physical activity. Only 58 percent of Americans actually engage in these activities.[5]

In my study of these things, I wasn't able to find any reputable statistics to point to the fact that Christians are any different. They are therefore just as sick, possibly dying prematurely because of poor health and therefore not around as long as they might have been to engage in kingdom work.

Watchman Nee admonishes the body of Christ in his classic *Journeying Towards the Spiritual*:

> Numerous Christians do not know how to glorify God in their eating and drinking. They do not eat and drink simply to keep their body fit for the Lord's use but indulge to satisfy their personal desires. We should understand that the body is for the Lord and not for ourselves; hence we should refrain from using it for our pleasure. Food ought not hinder our fellowship with God since it is to be taken purely to preserve the body in health.[6]

Ouch, Nee nails it, doesn't he? When you are a follower of Jesus, your body isn't yours—it's his. What we put into it, is his business. When we don't feed and fill it with helpful, healthy things, we will get crushed and getting crushed physically will undeniably have widespread effects in other areas of one's life. As a result, a seedbed for destructive habits may be born. In America, these habits often take the form of substance abuse, as indicated by the following statistics:

4. "Adult Obesity Facts," line 1.
5. "US Leads Overall Spend," lines 4–5, 34.
6. Nee, *Journeying Towards the Spiritual*, 210.

- 13.5% of Americans 12 and over used drugs in the last month, a 3.8% increase year-over-year (YoY).

- 59.277 million or 21.4% of people 12 and over have used illegal drugs or misused prescription drugs within the last year.

- 138.543 million or 50.0% of people aged 12 and over have illicitly used drugs in their lifetime.

- 138.522 million Americans 12 and over drink alcohol.

- 28.320 million or 20.4% of them have an alcohol use disorder.

- 25.4% of illegal drug users have a drug disorder.

- 24.7% of those with drug disorders have an opioid disorder; this includes prescription pain relievers or 'pain killers' and heroin.[7]

- Between April 2020 and April 2021, "nearly 92,000 people in the U.S. fatally overdosed on drugs."[8]

- 5.9 million Americans misused sedatives or tranquilizers in the past year."[9]

- During 2015–2018, 13.2% of adults aged 18 and over used antidepressant medications in the past 30 days.[10]

While these things might not be considered sinful in and of themselves, the addiction, or reliance upon them, leads to bondage, and bondage, or enslavement to a substance, person, habit, or force, other than God himself, is a prescription for death. C. S. Lewis, a lifetime hardcore smoker (he called himself a tobacconist) commented often about his early love for tobacco, ultimate enslavement to it, then related efforts to be freed from his addiction:

> "Smoking is much harder to justify, I'd like to give it up but I find this hard, i.e. I can abstain, but I can't

---

7. "Drug Abuse Statistics," lines 3-11.

8. Minkove, "New Research and Insights," lines 3–4.

9. Miller, "Sleep Medication Addiction Statistics," line 9.

10. Brody and Gu, "Antidepressant Use Among Adults," lines 1–2.

concentrate on anything else while abstaining—not smoking is a whole time job."[11]

Bottom line, what you feed grows, and the longer we let it grow, the more it has the potential to crush us. Whether it's smoking, overeating, drinking, or something else. Simply put, we are dirt (see Gen 1–2). What we plant in the dirt or soil of our lives will ultimately grow . . . and our physical existence is no exception. Good seed equals a good crop and bad seed a bad one. Good habits, diet, sleep, etc., yield the crop of a good, healthy, productive life. The opposite results in poor health, lack of energy, and potentially premature death. When our appetites drive us, God's intention for our whole health loses shape—often literally. We begin to lose ourselves in the pursuit of more. Habits and desires numb and fill us till we are bloated and blind to others. Jabba the Hutt, an infamous slug-like character in the original *Star Wars* trilogy, is the embodiment of gluttony. He is portrayed as a large, slimy crime lord that constantly fills his mouth or objectifies the women he purchased. In his mind, everything exists to fulfill his desires. More money, more food, more pleasure. And these pursuits led to his very timely death, strangled by the things he thought were enslaved to him.[12]

Unhealthy habits not only cause you to use others for your own pleasure (like Jabba), but they can also drive you to isolation as you neglect the relationships and responsibilities of life. In *The Lord of the Rings*, Smeagol, also known as Gollum, embodies this isolation. Although he once lived in society and had healthy relationships with family and friends, he was driven away because his desires caused him to harm others. When Smeagol's cousin found the one ring, the source of evil in the world, Smeagol killed him and took the ring for himself. He fled, living in the darkness of the mountains, forgetting even his own identity. The ring drove him mad, and he forgot his name. He became known as "Gollum" because of the gagging sound he made when under the influence

11. Lewis, *Letters of C. S. Lewis*, 267.

12. Lucas, *Return of the Jedi*.

of the ring.[13] Too many men become like this: fleeing the community God intended for them because of selfish pleasures, ultimately leading to the erosion of their identities.

It's Time for a Change

I say it's time to change. However, change doesn't come easy. Especially when you've become accustomed to your present shape. It may not be healthy, but you are used to it—used to getting crushed into a shape that is not God's intention for you. Can you hear them? Hear what you ask? The trumpets from the theme song to the movie *Rocky*. If you've never heard it before, go ahead and put the book down, dial it up, listen to it, and come back ready to knock out those things that are knocking you out. It's time to crush it. I remember the first time I watched Rocky Balboa get ready to fight his opponent, the heavyweight champion of the world, Apollo Creed. Rocky was an unknown barroom brawler who had no chance to beat Creed. However, his old sage of a trainer, Mick, led him into a new and unconventional rhythm. It would require focus . . . laser focus. It would entail the eating of raw eggs, chasing chickens, weird pushups and a myriad of other crazy preparations. So as not to spoil it for those of you who haven't watched the movie, suffice it to say, the eggs, chickens, and weird training techniques molded Rocky into a new shape. He became a formidable opponent for the overconfident Creed.[14] While the movie is a fictitious depiction of one man's epic journey from getting crushed by life and the bad habits that can often come with it, it also tapped into every man's real, epic desire to be strong, healthy, and available to do great things for his maker. Scripture gives us examples both of men who were crushed in their physicality and those who crushed their health to the glory of God.

13. Jackson, *Return of the King.*
14. Avildsen, *Rocky.*

Disciplined Disciples

Physical health and spiritual discipline are often connected in the Bible. Scripture records many heroes of the Old Testament remained physically healthy even to the end of their days. Moses and Caleb are two such examples:

> Moses was one hundred twenty years old when he died; his sight was unimpaired and his vigor had not abated (Deut 34:7).

> 10 And now, as you see, the Lord has kept me alive, as he said, these forty-five years since the time that the Lord spoke this word to Moses, while Israel was journeying through the wilderness; and here I am today, eighty-five years old. 11 I am still as strong today as I was on the day that Moses sent me; my strength now is as my strength was then (Josh 14:10–11, Caleb speaking).

Physical health is important because it allows us to serve God unhindered by limitations that we could have prevented. Sickness and disease may come even for the most disciplined, but the apostle Paul states in 1 Cor 6:19:

> Or do you not know that your body is a temple of the Holy Spirit within you, which you have from God, and that you are not your own?

Our bodies are temples of the Holy Spirit. To the best of our ability, we are to take care of our temples to honor him and the things he has entrusted to us. Our families, friends, work, and overall effectiveness for God's kingdom are impacted when we don't take care of business. Early church leaders were instructed not to be "addicted to wine" but rather be "self-controlled" (Titus 1:7–9). Too many Christians are too lazy to crush serpents. Instead, we crush couches, chips, and substances while our eyes are glued to a screen. The cross demands more dying-to-self than what we have made it.

Jesus Crushed His Health

Finally, Jesus is the ultimate serpent crusher with his health. Basic details tell us he crushed his physicality: he was a stone mason by trade, walked everywhere he went, and endured a brutal beating that would have killed most before being nailed to the cross. But it wasn't just what he did that caused him to crush his health; it was his lifestyle of discipline. Our Savior regularly separated himself from the crowds to fast and pray. Every meal he went without, every ache of hunger he endured was just another nail in the coffin of temptation. We all could use that type of focus to intentionally separate ourselves from a desire or need in order to pursue God's will. We can easily become dependent upon temporary things while our Lord invites us to release these to pursue him. He shows us that while some of the things of this world can be good, it is only when they are submitted completely to him.

CRUSH IT

C–Call on the Name of the Lord

Take a step back from your daily routine. Ask Jesus to show you what you are using to cope with life. Do you run to food? Do you run to a screen? Do you run to work? Surrender your habits to Jesus in prayer, even if you do not know what obedience to him in this area looks like yet.

R–Recall What He Has Done for You

Think back to moments or seasons in which you sought Jesus and did so with excellence. These could include healthy physical, emotional, or spiritual seasons. If you have trouble thinking of times like these, imagine what it would be like if you lived free of the things that are consuming your health. Imagine the time, energy, and purpose that are possible when you submit completely to Jesus.

U–Unleash the Authority of Heaven against the Serpent

Read Luke 2:52 out loud:

> *And Jesus increased in wisdom and in stature, and in divine and human favor.*

This verse speaks of how Jesus grew. We are called to follow and imitate him. Ask Jesus to guide you in living with the same excellence that he did. Pray specifically against any lazy and undisciplined habits in your life. Write down this verse and put the list somewhere so that you will see it regularly as a reminder of the Christ-like lifestyle that you have been called to as it relates to your body.

S–Stand

Prayerfully write down areas of your life that you recognize have not reflected Christ's lordship. Here are some examples that you could reflect upon:

- Physical health

- Mental/emotional health

- Spiritual health

- Relational health

Remember that these areas are intertwined, even though it may help to identify specific serpents as they relate to your health. After compiling this list, write down one tangible step you could take this week in each area. Steps could include a workout schedule, journaling in a notebook, or starting a new Bible reading plan. This intentionality is a great start towards seeing lasting change in the area of crushing the serpents that are crushing your body.

H–Hold the Line

> "For a habit to stay changed, people must believe that change is possible. And most often, that belief only emerges with the help of a group."[15]

Find a person or a group that will encourage and keep you accountable in these areas. Lasting change is much more likely to happen when we practice healthy habits in the context of community. Reach out to someone this week to discuss and pray about the list that you have created.

IT–Your Health

God is interested in every facet of your being and calls you to live in freedom. The serpent will take any opportunity to erode your health through compromise and yielding to temptation. An unhealthy life limits your effectiveness in God's Kingdom; therefore the conquest of self must be a priority.

15. Duhigg, *Power of Habit*, 92.

5

Crushing Your Mouth

Words are Power

"You're a doormat out there. He's mopping the floor up with you," Rex's wrestling coach would say. The coach had a gift for demeaning and shaming . . . especially towards Rex. The coach's demeaning voice still rings in Rex's ears almost forty-five years later. It shames him and casts a shadow that says that he doesn't ever do enough. Many, many men have had that demeaning coach or parent speak over them at pivotal times in their lives. John's mom had this way of clearing her throat that meant "how could you be so stupid as to not see what I am seeing right now?" Clay's dad would let him know on a regular basis that he was not even planned. "Your mom and I made a mistake," his dad would say. "Because of you, we had to get married before we planned to. Changed the whole course of our lives." Those words cut Clay deep. Rex, John, and Clay are all grown men now, and they have come into my office and recounted those stories. Voices from the past that still haunt, shame, and condescend to them. Words are powerful, aren't they? They can crush you, or they can catapult you into a future that is legendary.

A wise sage once told me something valuable as I recounted to him my story of an old voice that still whispered my name. It was an old voice towards which I had a deep anger. A voice that belonged to someone who was physically dead, yet their voice still rang loudly in my mind—in some ways, louder than when they were alive. The sage said to me, "My dear brother. That person is dead and in heaven at this very instant. If you were to bring the issue up to them, they wouldn't even know what you were talking about. Those hurts, pains, and past offenses don't exist in the kingdom. In the book of Isaiah, God states: 'For I am about to create new heavens and a new earth; the former things shall not be remembered or come to mind'" (Isa 65:17). The power of old words that once crushed me got crushed with the sage's proclamation. I began to see that there is a place in the kingdom where hurtful, hateful, and life-stealing words get crushed themselves. Kingdom power alive in kingdom words.

Why are words so powerful? I think that it's because they can directly affect your soul. They either nourish it or crush it. Whoever first coined the phrase "sticks and stones can break my bones, but names (words) can never hurt me" was an idiot. I'm not meaning to hurt anyone who has ever uttered that statement in an effort to try and help someone who has been hurt by someone's name calling, but it's true. Sometimes sticks and stones hurt a lot less than words. Bruises and cuts can heal with time, but words often have a way of injuring and leaving gaping holes and bruises in us that never heal. What you hear can either feed or damage your soul. What you see can also feed or damage you. Your eye is the window to your soul, and your ears are also a gateway as well. Jesus says so in Matt 6:22–23:

> 22 "The eye is the lamp of the body. So, if your eye is healthy, your whole body will be full of light; 23 but if your eye is unhealthy, your whole body will be full of darkness. If then the light in you is darkness, how great is the darkness!"

Jesus was making a powerful point that what you see and hear impacts what you think about, and what you think about affects your heart. Your thoughts get to the core of you. The right words and images can kindle a flickering serpent-crushing flame, while the wrong ones can put it out like a blustery, cold northern wind.

Old Fire-Filled Words

In Josh 14, an old battle-scarred warrior named Caleb remembered the right words—God's. They were the ones that Moses had spoken to him decades before after he had peered into the promised land. He had come back with one of only two positive reports out of twelve spies sent into the land. If God had said it, it was okay with Caleb. Caleb had been standing on the promise that was given to him when he was forty years old. He hadn't forgotten. Moses had promised him a portion of land. The word of the old prophet spoken to him on behalf of God. The word would be his. He took it to heart for his life. The word would be a legacy for his people. It was a word that would lead him to the mountain country of Horeb, where the tombs of his ancestors Abraham, Sarah, Isaac, Rebekah, Jacob, and Leah were located (Gen 23, 25, 49). There was however, one *huge* problem when the word about his property was originally given to him. There were giants living in it. They were living there when the promise was made, which is why the other ten spies gave a bad report. Undoubtedly, four decades later, it was populated with more giants; yet, when Moses's successor Joshua was handing out deeds to property, Caleb reminded him of his predecessor's promise. He reminded him with a comment that has reverberated for thousands of years: "Give me my mountain" (Josh 14:12). In passing, he does mention as a side note something about giants living there, but, on the word of God, he obviously didn't see them as that big of a deal. The property was his. End of story.

There is a scene in the movie *Silverado* that is one of my favorite movie scenes of all time. In it, a cowboy named Padin has been robbed by bandits of all of his belongings and left for dead in the scalding heat of the desert. His gun, hat, and horse were gone. As fate would have it, two men find him, dying in the desert. After giving him water, they place him on one of their horses and ride to a town called Silverado. After the men take Padin to a pawn shop to buy him an old piece of trash gun, some raggedy clothes that don't fit, and a misshapen hat, the men head to the local saloon. Upon entering, Padin sees a man wearing his hat. Calmly, he walks over to the man, who is playing cards and stares at him. The bystanders all push away from the table and Padin calmly says, "You're wearing my hat." The man, looking very guilty, says, "I don't know what you're talking about, mister. I won these fair and square in a card game." Undeterred, Padin says, "And I hope that isn't my six shooter and gun belt you're wearin'. Now stand up and give them back." Even if you haven't seen the movie you probably know what happens next. The thief makes the mistake of trying to draw on Padin, whom we find out is quick with a gun, even an old one purchased in a pawn shop. The bandit falls dead, and Padin takes his hat back. Wrong had been made right. It was his property, and Padin took it back. Caleb did the same thing. Like Padin, I'm sure that he let the giants know that they were in his house and on his land. The report about these events is found in Josh 14 and is rather concise. Kind of like Padin's gunfight:

> 13 Then Joshua blessed him and gave Hebron to Caleb son of Jephunneh for an inheritance. 14 So Hebron became the inheritance of Caleb son of Jephunneh the Kenizzite to this day, because he wholeheartedly followed the Lord, the God of Israel. 15 Now the name of Hebron formerly was Kiriath-arba; Arba was the greatest man among the Anakim. And the land had rest from war.

The final word is that Caleb went, took his mountain, and renamed it. He renamed it because the giant who used to be the greatest man in the land didn't live there anymore. The power of words is generational. Caleb took his mountain—God's mountain. The one promised to him forty years earlier. It would be the all- important high ground for his people. It was a place where the heritage of his people had rested, and it would be so again. It is where the verdant pastures of Shiloh quietly flowed. It was a place that he would ultimately give to his daughter and her giant-killing husband Othniel (Josh 15:13–19). No doubt his girl had heard him speak of God's word to him—them. The power of words is both temporal and eternal—affecting generations. Caleb chose to believe the good, powerful, long-lasting word of God. Moses had given him a word from heaven, then he showed his family what it looked like to live in the power of that word. His daughter would stand on it, as would her giant-killing husband. A word got deep into Caleb, his kids, and ultimately his grand-kids. The positive, Spirit-empowered words of God will always crush the negative ones. Which words will you believe? Which words will you utter? By which words will you live?

Naming, Shaming Words

A final word about the power of words and their potential sham-ing power—or not. Sometimes words that could crush, get thrust into a divine kingdom transfer, and get crushed themselves. These words have to do with the power of a name. Names can be power-ful, can't they? What do you think when I say "Judas"? Adolph? Nimrod? Osama? They are all words and bring up pictures and thoughts and sentiments in our hearts and minds. Have you met any Judases lately? I would venture to say not. In the Old Testa-ment there was a name for the ages—Jabez:

> 9 Jabez was honored more than his brothers; and his mother named him Jabez, saying, "Because I bore him in pain." 10 Jabez called on the God of Israel, saying, "Oh that you would bless me and enlarge my border, and that your hand might be with me, and that you would keep me from hurt and harm!" And God granted what he asked. (1 Chr 4:9)

This name Jabez literally means "pain," or "I bore you in pain." It would be like your mom naming you "Pain," and every time she called you in to eat dinner at night, she would say, "Oh Pain, time to come in for dinner, honey." Wow, what a crushing thought. So, Jabez could have allowed himself to become bitter, upset, and hate-ful towards his mother, God, and anyone that yelled "Pain" at him. But not Jabez. It seems that he actually allowed the word to propel him to ask God to bless him so much so that his name would be changed without even having to change the word. Sometimes God would actually give someone a new name: Jacob the deceiver was changed to "Israel," the one who struggles with God. In this obscure passage, Jabez didn't ask God to change his name, just to change the circumstances around him. To change them so radically that Jabez would be known for something totally different. God did exactly what he asked. He honored Jabez's prayer and expanded his boundaries and his holdings to legendary proportions. The power of asking God to get in the middle of ill thought or ill-intended words and rephrasing them in a way that only he can. Life-changing, course-altering, word-crushing.

Jesus Crushed it with His Mouth

While Caleb, Jabez, and others in the Bible learned the power of words and God's ability to crush them, even when they were not intended to bless, Jesus, as we would expect, was the ultimate word crusher. While he crushed words on a regular basis, one amazing example is found in Matt 4:1–11. In it we see the devil come to him in an effort to sway him from his purpose. So, he tempts him with words of power. He says that he will give Jesus all of the land that his eye could behold. Jesus, seeing the devil for what he was, and is, and ever will be, a twister and abuser of words, had a few choice words for him: "It is written!" (Matt 4:4).

We all know that the devil usually doesn't stop with only a few words, nor did he with Jesus. This time he tempted him with his physical appetites. Hungry and on a fast, the devil tried to deter him and tried to entice Jesus into doing some type of trick. Jesus had some words for him, and they were once again, "It is written . . ." (Matt 4:7). Are you seeing a rhythm here? The devil has words for us, sometimes totally absurd and sometimes twisted to even sound like God. Finally, in an effort to finish this thing and, in my opinion, try and get Jesus to avert going to the cross, he tempts him to throw himself down. Having none of it, Jesus once again reminds the devil of what the word really says and crushes the serpent's efforts to redefine him and/or redirect him with words. Jesus, the Word himself, spoke the word to the enemy and crushed him again: "It is written!" (Matt 4:10).

What words are you speaking . . . believing . . . twisting? Are you crushing it, or getting crushed with your mouth? Will it be the truth spoken of in the Word or the lies of the serpent?

Let's *crush it with our mouths.*

CRUSH IT

C–Call on the Name of the Lord

Before or during a conversation, take a mental pause. This could even be just for a second, but take that moment to invite Jesus into that conversation. Ask him to guide your words and to be the lens through which you receive words from others.

R–Recall What He Has Done for You

Recall the effect that the words of others have had upon you. Think specifically about an encouraging word or two that bolstered your faith. Reflect on the power of those words in your life.

U–Unleash the Authority of Heaven against the Serpent

Speak encouragement to others. Seek to build others up in the truth because of Christ's presence in you. When others speak negatively towards you, hold firmly to Christ's truth about you. Reflect on Eph 4:29:

> Let no evil talk come out of your mouths but only what is good for building up, as there is need, so that your words may give grace to those who hear.

Write this verse on a notecard or on your phone. Have it in a place this week where you will regularly see it, reflect on it, and be empowered by God's Spirit to live it.

S–Stand

Intentionally seek to grow in your words. Set a reminder to send an encouraging word to someone regularly. Leave an affectionate note for your wife, and compliment something specific about her. Give a friend a call just to encourage and pray for them. Greet that quiet neighbor that is difficult to approach.

H–Hold the Line

Surround yourself with people who crush their words in the name of Jesus. If you do not have one yet, prayerfully seek a mentor who will speak encouragement into your life. Do your part to create an encouraging culture in your spheres of influence.

IT–Your Mouth

The New Testament describes Jesus as "the Word." God has charged communication with the power for great good or for great evil. By surrendering our words to Jesus, we follow him in revealing God's life to ourselves and to others.

6

Crushing Your Mind

"Finally, beloved, whatever is true, whatever is honorable, whatever is just, whatever is pure, whatever is pleasing, whatever is commendable, if there is any excellence and if there is anything worthy of praise, *think* about these things."—The apostle Paul, Phil 4:8 (emphasis added)

Have you ever met a man who could be described as having the same energy as a heavy sigh? One who struggles to get out of bed, but to "struggle" signifies more effort than he is willing to give? Low energy and a numb mind are the only signs left of his gradual descent into himself. He is like sediment on the bottom of a sea. Like that proverbial frog in a pot of water that has slowly started to boil, but he cannot, does not hop out. He doesn't hop because lethargy and inactivity have slowly, incrementally made it impossible. It's like death by a thousand paper cuts. Depression and its evil cousins panic and anxiety are like that. They tighten their grip, sometimes even in a mockingly inactive way. The heart's fire leaves, only to return in the frenzied moments of panic and despair. I have met so many men in my almost four decades of ministry who fit one or more of these descriptions. They were being crushed, crushed in their thoughts, and eventually every other aspect of their lives. But the crushing often happened after seconds, led to minutes, led to hours, led to days, led to weeks, led to months, led to years, led to decades, led to—you get the picture.

Maybe you've met a man who seems to be pursuing the right things but in the wrong way. A man who places all of his identity in his work, family, or reputation. A man who spends most of his time wishing that he had more money, a better job, more fame, or more of anything and everything. He just wants more, more, more. It has been said that sin is an inappropriate response to an appropriate need. All of us have needs, but what should we do with them? Are they in their proper places? Are we responding appropriately to the right ones and ignoring or saying no to the wrong ones? Or maybe no to the right ones at the wrong time. We must learn to crush our needs, putting them in the proper order, or the inappropriate ones (or appropriate at the wrong time) will crush us—but how do we do this? First, I want to propose to you that we need to talk about them. Expressing them to yourself, your trusted friends, and most importantly, to your creator—the one who made you. That's because your ultimate need is him. He is the one who will help you to respond appropriately to the needs that he has actually put within you. So many men seem to shut down, never talking about their needs in a healthy manner. This often creates a situation that is ripe for destruction. A man's mind can be a place of rest when in faith it is submitted to the serpent crusher. That seed of serpent-crushing faith can work miracles in the mind. Without it, the serpent will try to take you out, wear you down, or speed up your life, so much so that you will burn out and/or give up. He doesn't really care how, and he certainly doesn't fight fair; he just wants to defeat you—pummel you—crush you. Your mind is literally a battlefield, with shrapnel flying around all over the place. You get to decide whether you will crush or get crushed there.

Not for Prophets: Jonah and Elijah

Men of God have been assaulted for thousands of years. Have you heard of the prophet Jonah? He was a man of God who was active about 800 years BC and was sent to the Assyrians, an evil and barbaric foreign nation. His mission was to declare God's judgment upon the Assyrians (Jonah 1:2), but in his seething anger and hatred towards them, afraid that they might repent and be saved (Jonah 4:1–3), Jonah ran then bought a ticket on a boat headed in the opposite direction. This disobedience led to him being identified by the sailors on said boat as the one responsible for a cataclysmic storm, so he was thrown overboard at his own bidding, to appease his God, the one who had in fact sent the storm (Jonah 1:7–17). Flailing in the ocean, he is summarily swallowed by a fish, repents while inside of the fish and is then vomited up on the beach, exactly where he was told to go in the first place (Jonah 2). After repenting for his anger and disobedience, Jonah obeys God then preaches a very short but effective sermon to the Assyrians, who repent—a national revival ensues (Jonah 3). The revival was so powerful that God's judgment did not rain down upon the evil culture for another 150 years. Jonah learned his lesson and therefore became an obedient and happy prophet—right? Wrong! The book of Jonah actually ends with the prophet angrily pouting and complaining to God on a hill overlooking Nineveh (Jonah 4:1–10). He was bitter and enraged at the fact that God hadn't killed everyone in the evil city. Jonah was angry at the gracious nature of a loving God towards all people. Instead of celebrating God's mercy, Jonah resented it. The Bible never explains whether or not Jonah's perspective changed. What a sad end to a miraculous rescue, a powerful sermon, and an ensuing revival. Anger and disobedience can sink you, crush your mind, and potentially ruin your perspective, right in the middle of a move of God.

Another example of a prophet struggling mentally is the story of Elijah. Nearly three-thousand years ago, the nation of Israel was in a dangerous place. God's people had entered the promised land under the leadership of Joshua, Caleb, and a few others who had, in faith, believed in God's promise (see the book of Joshua). Their enemies had to be driven out, not to mention several giants, about whom we've spoken in earlier chapters. However, after a few generations, things took a turn for the worse, when the Israelites asked for a king (see 1 Sam 8–9). They wanted to be like the other nations surrounding them. This eventually led to the disastrous rule of their first king, Saul (1 Sam 15). David, the giant slayer, would ultimately follow Saul, but his reign was far from perfect. After David, the nation slowly disintegrated into civil war, corrupt leadership, and misplaced loyalties. It was into this climate that the prophet Elijah was sent to proclaim God's word to King Ahab. Ahab was evil, disobedient, and a hater of God and his prophet Elijah. You can find the narrative of these events in 1 Kgs 17–19. Ahab, along with the help of his evil wife Jezebel (more pagan than him), led Israel to worship other gods, especially the Baals and Asherah (see 1 Kgs 16:29–34). In response to these evils, Elijah proclaimed that there would be a drought, making him a hated man and enemy of the state. Three years after his proclamation, the kingdom seed and the serpent seed clashed in epic proportion on Mount Carmel as Elijah confronted Ahab directly:

> "When Ahab saw Elijah, Ahab said to him, "Is it you, you troubler of Israel?" He answered, "I have not troubled Israel; but you have, and your father's house, because you have forsaken the commandments of the Lord and followed the Baals. Now therefore have all Israel assemble for me at Mount Carmel, with the four hundred fifty prophets of Baal and the four hundred prophets of Asherah, who eat at Jezebel's table." (1 Kgs 18:17–19)

The people of Israel and the prophets of the pagan gods met Elijah at Mount Carmel. The challenge was simple: whichever god sent fire from heaven, that was the true god. The pagans went first but to no avail. Their songs, incantations, and rantings were met with silence. Elijah's simple prayer and proclamation of God's sovereign power were answered with fire—a fire that consumed the offering he prepared—one which had been covered with water in an effort to show the overwhelming strength of God (1 Kgs 18:22–46) . Elijah must have felt like he was on top of the world, however that world came crashing down as the revival he had certainly hoped for didn't ensue. Instead, the evil, pagan Queen Jezebel put a hit out on Elijah. She cursed him and vowed that if she had not killed him in a specific amount of time, that she would die. Elijah's amazing victory had been turned into a fear-induced run for his life (see 1 Kgs 19:1–9). A dark, suicidal pallor came over the man of God—defeated, depressed, and alone. God didn't show up in the manner that Elijah thought he would, and he didn't know what to do.

Have you had these same thoughts come into your mind? Thoughts that had turned from sure and certain success into, "I'm not enough," "I'm all alone," "No one cares," "I deserve this," "It would be better if I was dead." God's men throughout the Bible all experienced these thoughts. You and I are no different. Mental and emotional weight can slowly constrict around us as the serpent's lies seem like the ultimate truth. Our own mind becomes our greatest enemy and we feel like we are ready to give up. We begin to believe the same crushing, constricting lies that Adam and Eve did. The hisses of the serpent that tell us that we get to determine our success and destiny—not God. And then when we act on those lies and start getting crushed, we want to die.

But lies they are, and God does not leave us under the crushing weight of them. Elijah's fearful run from the threats of Jezebel brought him to the end of himself, directly to the lap of God, in a secluded cave on Mount Horeb. Jezebel would be crushed by horses, her carcass ripped apart by wild dogs (2 Kgs 9:30–37). Elijah's gifts from God in the cave were food and sleep, interspersed with a series of miracles and ultimately a gentle whispering voice from heaven. A voice that would bring affirmation about his destiny and direction for his future (1 Kgs 19:9–21). God hadn't allowed him to be crushed to death, but only chased to life—life in and through interaction with him and his life-giving voice.

Jesus Crushed It in His Mind

While the prophets Jonah and Elijah were both not so perfect examples of crushing it in their minds, the perfect example is, was, and always will be Jesus. He was not some somber, religious man who only displayed divine seriousness. He was, is, and forever will be a man—the victorious, serpent-crushing, God man! He knows what it is like to experience incredible joy, crushing pain, and the entirety of the emotions that exist in the human condition. He wept for his friend Lazarus (John 11:35). The book of Hebrews tells us that Jesus endured the cross because of the joy that was on the other side of the suffering (see Heb 12:2). Luke 10:21 states that Jesus "rejoiced in the Holy Spirit. . ." In Matt 14:11–14, Jesus separated himself from the crowds when he found out that John the Baptist had been killed. It is quite possible that he needed time to himself to process and mourn the death of his cousin. He is an example to us that emotions are not to be ignored but to be considered and processed in relationship to God, the one who gave us our emotions in the first place.

Jesus would crush the potential for selfish desires throughout the entirety of his life. At the beginning of his ministry, he fasted and prayed for forty days in the desert (Matt 4:1–11). While there, the serpent tempted him with food, power, and fame, offering Jesus a quicker and easier solution in lieu of going to the cross—Jesus resisted. His mind was set on the Father's will, not his own.

Although there are countless other examples of Jesus crushing it in his mind, one of, if not the greatest instances of him doing so was on the night before he was crucified. As he prayed in the garden of Gethsemane, anxiety, depression, and the emotional weight of the sin of all mankind crashed down upon him. He knew his hour had come. He faced the most difficult, painful challenge any human has ever faced—bearing the weight of creation's sin via crucifixion. Scripture tells us that he sweat drops of blood as a result of his intense anguish (see Luke 22:42–44). Yet even in the face of this great turmoil, Jesus prayed: "Father, if you are willing, remove this cup from me; yet, not my will but yours be done" (Luke 22:42). Jesus crushed the serpent as it appealed to every ounce of his humanity—a humanity that didn't want to suffer on Golgotha. Yet Jesus the serpent crusher turned his face towards the cross and did what he was born to do: die so that all who would follow him might become serpent crushers as well.

CRUSH IT

C–Call on the Name of the Lord

When you are struggling with your thoughts, perception of self, perception of others, or emotions, take a breath. Out loud or in your mind, say "Jesus." Say Jesus' name slowly while focusing on him. Say his name again and again and again . . .

R–Recall What He Has Done for You

Reflect on the cross itself. Jesus' sacrifice was the greatest proof of your worth and the worth of others. Focus on the cross in the midst of your most challenging thoughts or emotions.

U–Unleash the Authority of Heaven against the Serpent

Constantly fill your mind with Scripture. This could be the same verse throughout the day, listening to longer passages in the car, and committing Scripture to memory based on the difficulties you are facing. Here are some examples:

To crush anger: Luke 23:34

> *Then Jesus said, "Father, forgive them; for they do not know what they are doing."*

To crush anxiety: Ps 23

> *The Lord is my shepherd, I shall not want. He makes me lie down in green pastures; he leads me beside still waters; he restores my soul. He leads me in right paths for his name's sake. Even though I walk through the darkest valley, I fear no evil; for you are with me; your rod and your staff—they comfort me. You prepare a table before me in the presence of my enemies; you anoint my head with oil; my cup over-flows. Surely goodness and mercy shall follow me all the*

days of my life, and I shall dwell in the house of the Lord my whole life long.

To crush laziness: 1 Cor 9:24

Do you not know that in a race the runners all compete, but only one receives the prize? Run in such a way that you may win it.

To crush worry about finances: Matt 6:25–27

Therefore I tell you, do not worry about your life, what you will eat or what you will drink, or about your body, what you will wear. Is not life more than food, and the body more than clothing? Look at the birds of the air; they neither sow nor reap nor gather into barns, and yet your heavenly Father feeds them. Are you not of more value than they? And can any of you by worrying add a single hour to your span of life.

Choose a passage and memorize it. Repeat it as a prayer whenever your mind is attacked in that area.

S–Stand

Eliminate or limit things in your life that hinder or hurt your mental health. These could include excessive amounts of social media, television, work, food, or time spent looking at your finances. Replace these with healthy habits such as exercise, reading, journaling, prayer, or a new hobby.

H–Hold the Line

Discuss the last two points with other believers, such as a mentor, pastor, or fellow Christian. Make it a normal habit to meet with that person to discuss these things for accountability and encouragement.

IT–Your Mind

You have been given the mind of Christ. Every sinful desire and broken mindset must submit to this fact. Remind all serpents of this by reciting the verse below as often as you need to complete the crushing process!

1 Cor 2:16:

> *For who has known the mind of the Lord so as to instruct him?' But we have the mind of Christ.*

7

Crushing your Sexuality

"Everything in the world is about sex except sex. Sex is about power."—Anonymous

"Thus we are caught in the perplexity that sex often represents both the best and the worst moments of our lives. While sex may at times create moments that mark our deepest shame, it can also make us feel more alive than ever before."—Gary Thomas, *Sacred Marriage*[1]

Y ou may or may not be old enough to remember the name Gary Condit. He was a US congressman who had a secret liaison with someone who wasn't his wife. She ended up getting killed, and it all blew up on him. And while he was never convicted of killing her, he was guilty of lying to his wife and being less than forthcoming in revealing the nature of his relationship with the young lady, Chandra Levy. If you don't remember Condit, just keep reading, because every generation has more than enough of these kinds of men—the ones who get crushed in the area of their sexuality.

Remember Congressman Anthony Weiner? Yes, he too was one who did less than admirable things in relation to his sexuality. He got caught taking pictures of himself naked and then sending them to someone who was underage on the internet. He too

1. Thomas, *Sacred Marriage*, 183.

was married, had kids and, was on the fast track to becoming the mayor of New York. How about Donald Trump? Yes, our former president. Not only has he been married several times, he too had some questionable relationships with women other than his wife, Melania, who happens to be very beautiful. He was also caught on tape saying foul, objectifying things about women. Does Dwight Eisenhower ring a bell? An amazing war hero and president he was, but he too had at the very least questionable relationships with someone other than his wife, Mamie. John F. Kennedy, the good-looking, legendary former president was also legendary for some of his extramarital exploits.

I can hear many of you saying, "Yeah, but they weren't men of God." Well, hold your horses—or pulpits, might I say. How about Jimmy Swaggart? Jim Baker and the list of preachers, pastors, and famous evangelists is every bit as long as the politicians who have messed up. Only recently the names of Ravi Zacharias and Carl Lentz have been added to the list of famous men of God who have gotten crushed in the area of their sexuality. I don't write about any of these men to poke fun or to enter into gossip or shame them. I am saddened for all of them, their families, and the innocent ones left in the wake of them getting crushed in the area of their sexuality.

If we are going to turn the tables and stop getting crushed in our sexuality, we have got to know what crushing it looks like, but before that, we need to examine in a bit more depth the sad truth about why men are so powerless in every generation. Remember the epic battle between the seeds of the serpent and the seed of the woman? Victory for men is tied very closely to their sexuality. How they steward their sexuality has a huge effect upon their ability to operate effectively in their roles as husbands, fathers, and, ultimately, leaders.

Jezebel is Still ALIVE, You Can Be DEAD Sure of It

Why are so many men so powerless, ineffective, and the source of much mockery and disrespect in every generation? I blame it on Jezebel. I know what you're thinking. We already mentioned her last chapter. She was the mad, powerful, pagan queen who opposed Elijah and died centuries ago. While true, her spirit lives on to lure, seduce, and intimidate many many men today. If you don't remember the story, Jezebel was the wife of King Ahab. Theirs was a marriage that was supposed to be an alliance to secure military favor with an enemy but was ultimately a sell-out to the seed of the serpent. Jezebel encouraged the worship of other gods and literally used governmental funds to sponsor priests who engaged in wild and nasty services to those gods. Pagan priests on the king's payroll. That is a recipe for disaster. Jezebel engaged not only in worship of her pagan gods, she intimidated the man who was supposed to be God's king, Ahab. Ahab was seduced by her, then intimidated as well. I am sure that she could be beautiful and alluring, but if she couldn't seduce you, she would crush you in other ways. She had her way with this king but ultimately met someone in the prophet Elijah who did not bow to her gods and ultimately defeated them on Mount Carmel by calling fire from heaven. After doing so, he then had all of the vile pagan priests executed. It was a brutal time in history. Although Jezebel may have initially thought she had the upper hand when Elijah went into hiding, she would ultimately be trapped in a siege by the next king of Israel. She was thrown from a window, her flesh to be eaten by dogs. A sad end—or was it?

Jezebel in the New Testament?

I say, "or was it," because Jezebel makes yet another appearance, not in the Old Testament, but in the new. Over two-thousand years after her supposed demise, she is mentioned by John, in the book of Revelation. In a letter to the believers in the city of Thyatira, John records this word: "But I have this against you: you tolerate that woman Jezebel, who calls herself a prophet and is teaching and beguiling my servants to practice fornication and to eat food sacrificed to idols." (Rev 2:20). Wow! There she is again. We're not sure if John was speaking about a woman who was a prophetess in the city of Thyatira or the old girl who put a hit out on Elijah. My personal opinion is that he was speaking of a demonic spirit that sought out men, especially God's men, and seduced and crushed them in the area of their sexuality. Think about it: there are so many men of God who use porn or are on the internet looking at things that they have no business looking at. One source states that "68% of church-going men and over 50% of pastors view porn on a regular basis. Of young Christian adults 18–24 years old, 76% actively search for porn."[2] There are also many men of God who engage in habitual masturbation, and I promise you that they are not thinking of nothing as they reach climax. In my opinion, Jezebel is alive and crushing so many who need to be crushing their sexuality—instead, they are getting crushed. Is there any hope? Absolutely.

What Crushing Sexuality Looks Like

But to learn how to defeat her in our day and age, we need to see what was done to defeat her in the Old Testament days. First, as we examine her ugly death, we see that she had first of all tried to seduce the men who would ultimately face her. This is how Jezebel rolls. She will try and seduce, and then, if she can't, she will try and steamroll you. This is what she tried with Elijah. There was no way that the man of God was going to be seduced by her, so she put a hit out on him and vowed to kill him violently. I think that it is important to note that it wasn't just one man who tried to take her out but a team of eunuchs. Now stay with me here. I am not saying that you must be a eunuch to overcome Jezebel, but I am saying that you should not face her alone. How many tragic stories I have heard as a pastor. Stories about guys who

2. "15 Stunning Statistics About Porn in the Church," lines 16–17.

enter into relationships with women who were not their wives, either in person or on the internet, and it ended terribly. Divorce, porn, fornication, and adultery. The eunuchs were a team, and you, me, and every other red-blooded man needs a team. Do not meet with Jezebel alone. I also need to make sure that you realize that I am not calling every woman Jezebel. I do, however, believe that the serpent can use female sexuality for his purposes and incites the same thinking and authority through some women that he used in, on, and through Jezebel.

I believe this because John speaks of it in Rev 2:22. He points out that men of God are sleeping with Jezebel. I don't think that this is only a metaphor either. I think that men are doing it in their minds via the internet, movies, music, and the images that live in their minds as a result of not protecting what goes into their thoughts. Our thoughts affect our bodies. This is what John was trying to say and it is an eerie tale that he prophecies in Rev 2. One that eerily seduces, kills, and robs so many men of their authority. In fact, John tells us that men will have no authority, no effectiveness. He says that their children will die, and ultimately they will have no authority in nations. That's the one that got me. I mean, when I read it the first time I thought, "if I don't get my sexuality in line and stop getting crushed in that area, I will be powerless." I don't know about you, but I don't want to get crushed in this area. I want to do the crushing.

Jesus Crushed His Sexuality

"Take a Drunk Girl Home . . ."

I remember the first time I heard the above statement. It was at the Grand Ole Opry, and Chris Janson was singing the song that he had written by that name. The religious part of me was initially piqued, and my antennae were on full alert. The song tells the story of a young woman who gets drunk at a party. In my mind I was thinking, "that girl shouldn't have been at the party in the first place," but the song took a different turn.

The gist of the song is that the girl has experienced a break-up, is depressed and drunk, and bounces around to bars and parties. A guy happens upon her and has a choice to make: sleep with her or take her to her house, put her in bed, and assure that she's safe. He chooses the latter.

It was absolutely powerful. I would want that too, and I would also want to be that guy and especially raise sons who were that guy. This is the kind of guy that the serpent crusher was, is, and can empower you to be. He can help us to become men who don't get enticed in the place where our basest nature gets lured into a disempowering predicament.

And Don't Objectify a Naked One

To objectify something means to use it like an object. Jezebel had painted up her face, attempting to entice the men who eventually did away with her (2 Kgs 9:30–33). It was her nature. Now I am not in the slightest encouraging men to do harm to a woman like these men did (i.e., pushing her out of a window), but I am saying that Jezebel's alluring call to sleep with her and have sex with her literally or even mentally (i.e., on the internet) is still something that is very real and must be dealt with. So, take the drunk girl home, and don't give in, and use the naked, scantily clad, or alluring one. This may seem very difficult, but the serpent crusher is able to help you. I know he can. I am sure that he was approached by many women in his day. There were Lazarus's sisters, Mary and Martha, Mary Magdalene who Jesus rescued from demonic oppression, the woman at the well in John 4, the woman who washed his feet with her hair in Luke 7 and the infamous woman caught in adultery in John 8. I encourage you to read more of each of their stories. In none of these relationships do we see a hint of Jesus objectifying these women. In fact, we see the total opposite. I am sure that he probably would have had the opportunity to appease his natural desires, and the serpent who controlled Jezebel would have loved to see him give in. But he didn't. Not once. And since he didn't, he can empower you to stand strong too (see Heb 4:14–16).

My favorite story dealing with Jesus' ability to stand strong and not objectify a woman is found in John 8. It was a total set-up from the beginning. A woman was caught in adultery, with no mention of the man. She had been set up; the man had been given a pass because boys will be boys, you know. I hate this excuse. Stop using it! It is immature and needs to be done away with. Jezebel and the serpent love to use it and appeal to it in the lives of millions of men every day. Well, if you want to stand, and if you want to be a real man and become the seed of the serpent crusher, you will need to act like a man and stop objectifying women. Back to our story. After being set up, the woman is dragged into the street to be embarrassed and stared at by Jesus and the other men. These guys were religious wimps, hiding behind one another and their religion, but still getting to look at a naked woman. Or at least listen to the adultery that had been going on. This is voyeurism at its worst. They ask him what he was going to do. They had caught this woman in the act. Would he stone her? She could have gotten the death penalty in their culture, and he, the perfect one, could have inflicted the penalty. But what does he do? He tells the religious authorities that the one who was without sin could throw the first stone.

Like a wall, Jesus deflected the guilt and shame they meant to use as a weapon against the woman. The guilt and shame now rained down on them through the truth of Jesus' pointed statement. In that moment, Jesus had become a wall for his daughter.

Not one of them could so much as pick up a pebble. They were frozen. While they were trying to figure a way out of that awkward moment, Jesus bent back down and continued to write in the dirt. Eventually, the self-righteous mob of knuckleheads dispersed. Ironically, they were chased away by the only one present worthy of actually picking up a stone and hurling it at the woman, the only one present without sin. But instead of picking up a stone he became a stone, a whole manly wall of them. Jesus wasn't about peeping and sneaking around trying to catch people in dirty traps. He preferred to look them straight in the eye with a look that at the same time chased away religious traffickers while comforting a hurting woman. Comforted, covered, protected, loved, and sent off to live a better life. This woman, and millions like her down through time, was someone's daughter. She was his daughter. I pray that God would help us all get rid of those ugly ways we relate to women. No more peeping, hoping for a perverted momentary thrill. No more objectifying, manipulating, or using. I pray that we would be moved by the Holy Spirit to step in front of women to be a wall of covering and protection, creating a safe place where they can live, grow, love, and hope.

Jesus can help us renew our minds. How? Jesus was a man. He had the same genetic makeup as we do. He had the capability to think sexual, sensual thoughts. But unlike us, he never, ever sinned. The writer of the book of Hebrews reminds us,

> For we do not have a high priest who is unable to sympathize with our weaknesses, but we have one who in every respect has been tested as we are, yet without sin. (Heb 4:15)

Thank you, Jesus! He was tempted to sin but never did. Let me say it again. Jesus was tempted, just as we are. But he never sinned! He did not objectify women. He did not touch them sinfully. He did not fantasize about them. He lived a perfect, healthy, balanced, manly, and sinless life. He is the perfect one to give us the capacity to live in that victory just as he did.

With his resurrection, he sealed the ultimate victory over everything that would ever plague the masculine body, soul, and spirit. Jesus saves our entire nature, including the way we think and interact with women. That includes our mothers, our wives, our female coworkers, women on computer screens, women in church services, and women walking down the street.

If you've struggled in this area as I have, you should fall on your knees right this minute and ask Jesus to save you, and ask him to give you his heart for all women. When this happens, and it will happen if you ask for it, you will receive a whole new nature. You'll gain not just a new way of thinking; you'll gain a new way of being. Remember what the apostle Paul said:

Therefore, if anyone is in Christ, the new creation has come; The old has gone, the new is here! (2 Cor 5:17)

Take it from a guy who's been there. You can be delivered from your knuckleheaded nature. Your mind can be renewed in this area. And as you know, if you get your mind right, the right actions will follow. And when your actions are right, your life can change. This kind of change is especially important in the midst of a hyper-sexualized, voyeuristic culture.

If we ever hope to be the wall of non-knuckleheaded manhood that God created us to be, we're going to have to pattern our lives and our nature after his. We must learn to touch others the way he touched them, with humility and healing, not with selfish intent.

Lord Jesus, I ask you to teach us to reach out and touch the women in our lives the way that you would have us touch them. I pray that we would learn to love, honor, and respect them the way you do, because they are your daughters; they are your daddy's girls.

CRUSH IT

C–Call on the Name of the Lord

When your thoughts and heart rate begin to speed up in the presence of sexual temptation, slow yourself down. If possible, remove yourself from a compromising situation by going outdoors or somewhere public. Speak the name of Jesus over your mind and desires.

R–Recall What He Has Done for You

If you are married, remind yourself of your spouse and the gift that they are to you. Think back to the pure joy it is to be in God's presence without guilt or shame. Reflect on the honor that it is to be God's child and the sacrifice Jesus made for you to be clean.

U–Unleash the Authority of Heaven

Choose a Scripture to be your battle verse. Whenever tempting thoughts come to mind, repeat that Scripture several times. Here are some examples of verses you could commit to memory for this:

2 Tim 2:22

> *Shun youthful passions and pursue righteousness, faith, love, and peace, along with those who call on the Lord from a pure heart.*

1 Thess 4:3–8

> *For this is the will of God, your sanctification: that you abstain from fornication; that each one of you know how to control your own body in holiness and honor, not with lustful passion, like the Gentiles who do not know God; that no one wrong or exploit a brother or sister in this matter, because the Lord is an avenger in all these things, just as we have already told you beforehand and solemnly warned you. For God did not call us to impurity but in holiness. Therefore whoever rejects this rejects not human authority but God, who also gives his Holy Spirit to you.*

1 Cor 10:13

> *No testing has overtaken you that is not common to everyone. God is faithful, and he will not let you be tested beyond your strength, but with the testing he will also provide the way out so that you may be able to endure it.*

2 Cor 10:3–4

> *Indeed, we live as human beings, but we do not wage war according to human standards; for the weapons of our warfare are not merely human, but they have divine power to destroy strongholds.*

Eph 5:11–14

> *Take no part in the unfruitful works of darkness, but instead expose them. For it is shameful even to mention what*

> *such people do secretly; but everything exposed by the light becomes visible, for everything that becomes visible is light.*

S–Stand

Identify your areas of weakness and make a plan to fight temptation in that area. If you struggle with sexual temptation on the internet, look into accountability software such as Covenant Eyes. Throw out every pornographic magazine, video, or picture you have in your house. Delete any hookup apps you have used for sexual experiences. Identify the most common times, places, and situations in which you fail sexually through masturbation. Write down a specific plan on how you will flee temptation when it arises. For example, you could:

1. Remove yourself from the tempting situation by going on a run, meeting up with a friend, or at least going to a different room.

2. Repeat your memory verse out loud or in your mind.

3. Engage in physical activity like push-ups, sit-ups, etc. to burn some energy.

4. Reach out to someone you are honest and accountable to through a call or text.

H–Hold the Line

Community is incredibly important in sexual purity. We can't do this alone. Find a believer in your life who you can be honest with and who has experienced victory in this area themselves. Share your thoughts from the last point and ask them to be your accountability partner in the areas you struggle with. Furthermore, here is a list of books that are great resources for living in purity:

- *Defending the Feminine Heart* by Jeff Voth

- *Clean* by Doug Weiss

- *Every Man's Battle* by Stephen Arterburn

IT–Your Sexuality

The serpent wants to see the gift of sexuality perverted from its original intent.

This area can be one of the greatest gifts or greatest weaknesses in the life of a man. When submitted to God, sexuality worships the Father and proclaims the beauty and wholeness of his kingdom.

8

Crushing Your Heritage

"Who. can give a man this, his own name? God alone! For no one but God sees what the man is . . ."—George MacDonald[1]

What Getting Crushed Looks Like

One day within earshot of my kids, someone said, "Uh oh, they're pastor's kids, you know what that means . . ." It was all I could do to keep from crushing them. But because that isn't usually what pastors do to their sheep, I restrained myself. But this one needed crushing—at least their words did. He was relating what has been said over and over again. That is that pastors' kids end up being the worst and most rebellious ones. I hate that sentiment. While I know many pastors' kids who aren't the hellions that this ignorant sheep was trying to speak over my kids, I must admit that what they were trying to speak over my kids does happen more often than I would like to admit. It also points towards the power of one's heritage. The enemy thinks enough of that power to do anything that he can to steal it. He had a plan for Adam and his kids in the garden, didn't he? In fact, he spoke against Adam's father, the creator himself. He inferred that his daddy had lied to him and that maybe it was okay for him and his wife to disobey

1. MacDonald, "Meditation on Becoming a Self."

their dad and eat the fruit. We all know how that ended up, don't we? Apple eaten, heritage stolen, and the entirety of the story of the Bible is the ensuing battle between the seed of the serpent and the seed of the woman. A brutal assault on the heritage of every man, woman, and their children since the original apple was eaten and the seed of disobedience nurtured. Heritage means "something transmitted by or acquired from a predecessor: legacy."[2]

Generational Curses?

I don't know what your theology is in regards to generational curses, but I think that they're a thing—a real thing. Whether or not you believe they are spiritual, genetic, emotional or a combination of all of them, you have to admit that there is something going on in some families. You may have said it, or you may be one of the families that it's spoken about. "Those people in that family always—you fill in the blank. His daddy was a something, his granddaddy was a something, and he will be a something too. You can fill in what kind of something. To a certain extent, that's true, unless a change is made. A crushing change. Are you tired of getting crushed?

Tom was crushed. He was on the verge of divorce because of secret sexual compromises. One day in my office, he began to recount a story where he remembered his dad cheating on his mom. As a little boy he was devastated. He was cut to his heart. Then, as he watched his parents fight and their marriage disintegrate before him as he grew into manhood, he vowed that he would never do what his dad did. He grew bitter and upset. But you know what, he was doing the same thing. His marriage was a mess, and he didn't know what to do. And now he had two sons and a daughter in the house watching him. He was repeating the very sins he swore he would avoid.

2. "Heritage," line 2.

Spiritual, Mental, and Emotional Effects

Think about the spiritual, mental and emotional effects upon those watching you. Statistics are staggering when it comes to the effects of the habits of a parent upon their children. Children of criminals are almost twice as likely to become criminals themselves.[3] Those who had unfaithful parents are two and a half times more likely to be unfaithful in their relationships.[4] However, these statistics do not mean that any person is guaranteed to follow in their parents' footsteps, but it is something to be aware of. Positively, fathers and mothers can set great examples that also make it more likely for their children to crush every area of their lives. When parents are on the same page, it can be powerfully synergistic. Synergistic in a good way or in a bad one. Synergy works generationally too.

Let's see if there is any merit to this generational theory in an historical context. Does the name Saddam ring a bell? He was the famous, or infamous, dictator of Iraq that ruled through fear, secret police, and unprovoked violence against nearby nations. His sons, Uday and Qusay, followed their father in brutality for those that opposed them, though both were killed by American soldiers. Saddam himself was eventually cornered, put on trial, and hanged for his crimes.[5] See what I mean? Let's try another one. King Herod, the Roman-appointed ruler of Judaea when Jesus was born. Playing to the desires of the Roman Empire, Herod rose to power over any other contenders. He was paranoid and brutal in his old age, murdering his wife and her family from his suspicions, as well as ordering the execution of the infants in Bethlehem when Jesus was born.[6] His son, Herod Antipas, appears several times in the Gospels, but never for a good reason. He beheaded John the Baptist and later handed Jesus back to Pilate after Jesus would not perform a sign for him.[7] How about one more? Kim Jung-Il,

---

3. Besemer et al., "Systematic Review and Meta-Analysis," 161–78.

4. Brenner, "My Partner's Parents Cheated," lines 124–125.

5. "Saddam Hussein," lines 4–6, 80–82.

6. Perowne. "Herod, King of Judaea," lines 1–8.

7. "Herod Antipas," lines 1–9.

the former leader of North Korea, and his son Kim Jung-Un, the current leader of North Korea. Both were dictators with complete power who regularly eliminated those they saw as threats, including family members, and prioritized military strength over the basic necessities of their citizens.[8]

While there are some notorious gangsters and criminal types that end up with good kids, quite often the sins of the father are repeated by their sons and their daughters. Family after family gets crushed and crushed and crushed again. So, whether you are on the side of nature or nurture, heritage is dramatically affected by the presence of a father. What's a man to do? In many cultures, the man has three roles: protect, provide and discipline.[9] Men cover their children physically, emotionally, and spiritually. Men provide a safe environment for children to grow, explore, play, and learn who God has called them to be. Men show their children right from wrong and teach them how to live out the truth of God's Word. Well, succinctly stated—*show up*. Yes, show up and realize the inherent power you possess in being a man. Some of you reading this right now aren't fathers yet, but odds are, you will be. And even if you don't become a biological father, you can still use your manhood for the kingdom and help father those whom God brings into your life. While we don't have space in this chapter to print the entire article from which this next quote is taken, I encourage you to consider reading all of it. In it, J. Neil Tift goes a long way towards informing you about the power of your manhood. Power to either build up or tear down the children with whom you will come into contact.

> "... when fathers interact with their children, they are hardwired to prepare their children for the future ... This focus on the future is just hardwired in engaged fathers."[10]

A powerful statement, isn't it? Convicting, encouraging, and enlightening. My brother, you are hardwired to prepare your

8. Murray, "Kim Jong-Un," lines 46–55.

9. Tift, "Father's Place," line 56.

10. Tift, "Father's Place," lines 43–49.

children for the future. What kind of future are you instilling in them? Speaking over them? Modeling them? Living with them?

Take Your Name Back

Do you remember Jabez from chapter five? He took his name back, didn't he? By turning to God and engaging him in the process, then following after him in wholehearted obedience, his name was turned into something that forever stands as something totally different than it did originally. Moses was another of those biblical examples of turning his failed name and reputation into something new, hopeful, and eternal. He was a shamed murderer (Exod 2:11–12) and stutterer (Exod 4:10) who ultimately became a friend of God and, on his behalf, confronted the most powerful man on the planet, Pharaoh Ramses II. Moses would eventually become known for being a deliverer second only to Jesus. In the New Testament, the impulsive disciple Peter stated oracles from heaven that were praised by Jesus himself at one moment, yet only moments later was rebuked and called Satan (Matt 16:22–23). Peter's list of blunders is actually too long to include here, yet he would ultimately be chosen by his Lord to be the foundational leader tasked with establishing his church. Finally, there was Saul of Tarsus. He was the radical Pharisee empowered to stamp out the new movement of Jesus followers called "The Way" (Acts 7:58, 8:1–3). A movement that he was well on his way to crushing, until he got crushed himself on the road to Damascus (Acts 9:1–31). Such a smashing interaction that he would ultimately change his ways, follow Jesus, and, like Jabez, his name took on a new meaning. He would be known as the apostle Paul (Acts 13:9) and summarily write two-thirds of the New Testament, finally ending his race as a martyr under Emperor Nero. This is only a short list of those who followed the Lord and took their heritage back—personally, for their families and the kingdom. While each of these stories are unique in their own ways, there is one common thread—it is the thread of the serpent crusher. A thread that we have followed throughout the entirety of Scripture. A thread that actually comes to a powerful culmination in the book of Revelation 2:17. In this text, Jesus speaks to the ones who have followed him wholeheartedly—those who are named for him and by him. Meaning that it is for him that they exist, and he is the one who gets to call them what he wants to call them. No one else has this right:

> Let anyone who has an ear listen to what the Spirit is saying to the churches. To everyone who conquers I will give some of the hidden manna, and I will give a white stone, and on the white stone is written a new name that no one knows except the one who receives it.

What a powerful exclamation. Your past failures and circumstances don't get to name you—Jesus does. The white stone is believed to be an invitation or ticket to a special occasion, upon which there seems to be a name, a new one that only the host and the one receiving the invite will know. Some scholars think that this "new name" might be some kind of "pet name" or nickname that would be special and affirming.[11] It also suggests that the one receiving the name needs to get so close to the giver of the name that it could be whispered secretly. Jesus wants to affirm you closely—so much so that it's between only you and him. That sounds like something Jesus might do, doesn't it? He was famous for changing people's names, lives, and ultimate trajectories.

A Lion Awaits You

What will you choose to do? A decision must be made. It's your name, your heritage, and your future. You are in the middle of a battle, stones flying, shrapnel in the air, and standing there could get you killed and with you, the hope that lives within you—or, you can decide to be the better man that you were created to be. You are just one decision away. I want to encourage you to move forward with one final "take back what's yours" story, and it's found in 1 Chron 11:22. It has to do with a lion on a snowy day, and if it weren't in the Bible, I wouldn't believe it. It's the story of

11. "Revelation 2," verse 17.

a man named Benaiah. He was a valiant warrior and quite adept at fighting men, giants, and lions. The story says that he went into a pit with a lion on a snowy day, and he summarily killed that lion. Why would someone do that? There is no logical reason, unless maybe that lion had wandered onto his property, and he had heard him hiding there, laying in wait for an innocent victim. Maybe he had already harmed someone, but who wants to take on a lion? Especially if the weather is bad, and on a snowy day to boot? Obviously Benaiah did. He went into the pit, took care of business, and made it safe again. That was one lion who was not going to intimidate, harm, or pursue anyone anymore. Oh, and by the way . . . He also killed a giant Egyptian and took his spear from him. The text doesn't spend a lot of time elaborating on the exact circumstances; it's like it was another day at the office for him. I don't know about you, but I'll bet you got fired up by all of these stories, didn't you? The fictitious story of Padin taking his gear back and the real heroes, Caleb and Benaiah, crushing the opposition on the pages of the Bible. I think that men love these accounts because they stir something in us. They reach a place in us as men that stirs me to say, "I'm tired of getting crushed, and something needs to be done about it." I am here to tell you that there is hope for every one of us. Maybe you've been crushed in the past, but today is a new day and there have been some serpent-crushing, giant-killing, lion-pounding men in the past from whom we can learn tactically. The ultimate serpent crusher, Jesus, especially has something to teach us about taking our heritage back. All of these biblical examples were merely pointing towards him. They were imperfect men, doing miraculous things and feats, giving all of us hope. Hope that getting crushed is not what needs to be your normal anymore, but crushing it is.

Jesus Crushes Heritage

Jesus' heritage is ours. In Matt 1 and Luke 3 we can trace his ancestry all the way back to the beginning. He was the seed of a woman. While not entirely a Son of Adam, he was fully human, being born of Mary. He was also the heaven-sent seed to walk through all of the generations preceding him and come to this planet . . . to establish an entirely new lineage. One that would not fail and, by faith, be available to everyone who would follow him. That's what the lineage means to you and to me. The book of Hebrews gives many of the names of those who chose to follow him by faith, even before he came (Heb 11–12). He was that promise from Gen 3:15 and the serpent crushers who went before him chose to believe the God who said that he would come and follow him based on the Word of God. Then, Jesus was miraculously born, just like it said he would be in Micah 5:2. He would live in a human's house, Joseph and Mary's. He would grow up in his identity, knowing to whom he belonged. In fact, we can see this in Luke 2:41–52 when he got lost on a family trip to the city and ended up in his Father's house, the Temple. He knew his heritage. He knew his name. In John 8:58 he asserts the name in a unique and powerful way. He says, "Before Abraham was, 'I am.'" This is strong language. Throughout his ministry he would refer to himself as the Son of Man (Matt 26:64). He would assert that he was the way, the truth and the life (John 14:6). There is no doubt that he knew who he was, whose he was, and what he was called to accomplish.

Jesus would *crush* his heritage and so can you.

CRUSH IT

C–Call on the Name of the Lord

Whenever you start to believe that your identity or actions are more influenced by your family than by Jesus, repeat this prayer in your mind or out loud: "Jesus, I need your help to redeem my heritage." Repeat this prayer five, ten, twenty times.

R–Recall What He Has Done for You

The greatest proof that you are a new creation is the cross. Think about the payment Jesus made for you and how that payment supercedes any other curse, habit, or identity. Who are you in him? What has he brought you out of? Who do you want to be in him?

It may help to write your thoughts down from this section and keep that note as an encouragement for yourself in the future. When you struggle in this area, read the note again.

U–Unleash the Authority of Heaven against the Serpent

Read 2 Cor 5:17 out loud:

> *So if anyone is in Christ, there is a new creation: everything old has passed away; see, everything has become new!*

Write this verse down and put it where you will see it every day. Read it slowly, thinking about each word. Commit it to memory. Remind yourself and others of their newness in Jesus. Remember that this truth is greater than any physical or family tie.

S–Stand

Identify the voices that you are listening to. Are there people in your life that constantly remind you of who you used to be, or who your family is? Are there people in your life who regularly put you down? Has isolation led to your thoughts spiraling out of control? Identify the times and situations that lead you to accepting a heritage and messages that aren't from Jesus. Ask God how you can limit these destructive interactions, while encouraging ones that will lift you up and point you towards him.

H–Hold the Line

Share the previous points with another believer or group. Invite brothers and sisters into this process of walking in Christ's new life. As stated above, prioritize encouraging others in their struggles. Sometimes we can get so caught up in our own thoughts and issues that we lose sight of the things God wants to do through us.

IT–Your Heritage

Legacies can be a very powerful or a very destructive thing. The momentum of good and bad decisions reverberates throughout generations. Through the life of Christ, we are called and equipped to stop every curse and lay a foundation of faithfulness for those who will come after us. Think of them.

9

Crushing Death

"I am the resurrection and the life."
—Jesus Christ, John 11:25.

"Do not weep; for she is not dead but sleeping."
—Jesus Christ, Luke 8:52.

"He who learns to die daily while he lives will find it
no difficulty to breathe out his soul for the last time."
—Charles Spurgeon[1]

"Jacob's dead?" I heard my wife say in response to our daughter, who was on the other end of the call. Shock set in immediately—slowing reality down in my mind, while speeding up my heart—a God-given aspect of humanity that allows us to try and process that which we are seeing, hearing, and feeling that is life-shattering. What we were hearing was that our son Jacob had relapsed. He had gotten ahold of some heroin that was laced with fentanyl, shot up in the bathroom, then died—yes, died. To say that we were stunned was an understatement. He had collapsed on the ground in the parking lot of a local shopping mall. EMTs and police officers responded to a passerby's 911 call, loaded Jacob's lifeless body into an ambulance, and he was taken to a local

1. "10 Spurgeon Quotes," lines 26–27.

hospital. We were two hours away, traveling back from a track meet in which another of our sons had competed.

It was the day before Easter. The next two hours on the highway seemed like an eternity. Death stared us in the face while we stared at the pavement. It felt like it was laughing at us—death that is. That's what death does. It likes to get the last laugh. It has been that way since Adam and Eve invited it into their story, there in the garden, via the author of death, the serpent himself. Death and its crushing effects—life-crushing, breath-stealing effects. That's what the curse brought upon us. We have been tracking the story of the battle between it and the hope that resides in the seed of the woman. But, make no mistake, death will take its shots and get in its blows. That's the story of Scripture. The epic battle between the life of God and the death of the serpent.

Now back to our story—Jacob's story. Well, he's alive. Yes, I said it—*alive*. He was dead, but somewhere between the parking lot and the hospital, he woke up. Dead for 10–12 minutes, then woke up. Yes, the EMTs and ultimately the medical personnel at the hospital administered life-saving treatments, but we feel that there was much more going on that day. The prayers of his family, others who knew him, and rallying kingdom forces crushed death that day. A collective force of faith-filled people who stood against the shocking shadow. That's what we hope for, fight for, and stand for. We fight against the intimidating message, effects, and power of death. While death is real and its power ominous, the power of God is way more so.

Although we were given our son back from the grave, there are many that don't see this same result. Sometimes, even in the presence of prayer and faith, we see death. In many of the psalms we see the reality of death yet are continually pointed towards the hope of life in God. In Ps 139, David states, "Where can I go from your spirit? Or where can I flee from your presence? If I ascend to heaven, you are there; if I make my bed in Sheol [the realm of the dead], you are there." Again, David tells us in Ps 16:10–11, "Therefore my heart is glad, and my soul rejoices; my body also rests secure. For you do not give me up to Sheol, or let your faithful one see the Pit. You show me the path of life. In your presence there is fullness of joy; in your right hand are pleasures forevermore." God is our refuge, hiding place, and ultimate light that overpowers the shadow of death. Death is only a shadow for those who hope in God. Albeit present, cold, and real, there is a greater and more present reality—God himself. He is a light that makes death a shadow—a refuge that hides those who would dwell there.

The writer of Hebrews points to those in the Old Testament who battled death and did so in faith, looking to Jesus. Hebrews 11 lists several people who held firmly to God's promises, even though they didn't know the fulfillment of those promises like we do. These individuals include Noah when he built the ark (Gen 6), Abraham when he left his people to follow God (Gen 12), and Moses when he led God's people to the promised land (Exod 12). The author of Hebrews states that God's people had remained faithful to the Lord in the face of persecution and death even though they had not seen the full picture. This section of Hebrews ends with this:

> "Yet all these, though they were commended for their faith, did not receive what was promised, since God had provided something better so that they would not, apart from us, be made perfect. Therefore, since we are surrounded by so great a cloud of witnesses, let us also lay aside every weight and the sin that clings so closely, and let us run with perseverance the race that is set before us, looking to Jesus the pioneer and perfecter of our faith, who for the sake of the joy that was set before him endured the cross, disregarding its shame, and has taken his seat at the right hand of the throne of God. " (Heb 11:39-12:2)

The faithful ones of the Old Testament looked forward to the serpent crusher we now know: Jesus Christ.

Unless?

Throughout this book, we have looked at stories of ones who have crushed it and gotten crushed, and to tell you the truth, for all of the success stories, I promise that every earthly, serpent-crushing giant slayer got crushed at some point or another, because he was a mere human. All humans will ultimately get crushed . . . unless. Unless what, you ask? Unless you get coached up and helped by the ultimate serpent crusher himself. He is the one who never got crushed and stayed there. In fact, he chose to get crushed, not because he was weak or flawed but because that was his purpose from the beginning. He was the seed of the woman, born to assault the seed of the serpent and do it in dramatic fashion. So dramatic that it would reverberate through eternity. He would even choose the place where he would get crushed and then totally change the narrative. He came to the planet in a prophesied location (see Mic 5:2), lived in a prophesied manner, and entered into the epic tale that we have been looking at in each of the lives of each of the earthly serpent crushers. They helped him get here. They were involved in bringing the epic crusher to the planet, at the right time. That's what his lineage is there for. It is there to let us know that each generation pushed the seed forward until what Paul would call "the fullness of time" (see Gal 4:4–5) occurred. That terminology is actually pregnant woman terminology. When time was pregnant, he came, and the showdown occurred. The seeds would collide in one final showdown. In a specific place and a specific time.

Jesus' life pointed towards an ultimate confrontation with the giant serpent called death. The epic battle between the seed of the woman and the seed of the serpent. It's the battle that the whole Bible points to and focuses upon. Death, like a slithering python, exists to wrap its coils around you and crush the life from your body. Adam got crushed, Abraham got crushed, David got crushed . . . Every son of every son got crushed too. Periodically there would be a prophet who would remind the people that there was another narrative at work here, however. The seed would go forward, and periodically an awesome serpent-crushing, giant-slaying event would occur. Just to remind them. That was what the Old Testament was all about.

Then in the New Testament, the lineage of Jesus in Matt 1 and Luke 3 recount those generations. They tell the story of the seed coming to the planet to finish this thing. It was like the O.K. Corral, Anzio Beach, Normandy, and every other epic battle rolled into one, and it culminated on the hill where a head was displayed. Do you remember how we talked about Goliath's head in chapter two? What an epic way for God to show off through Jesus. The Son was impaled upon a pole where Goliath's head had once stood as a reminder of the battle that raged. Jesus would hang on that pole, just as it had been prophesied and pointed to for thousands of years. And when he uttered "it is finished," the battle was ultimately almost over—almost. The apostle Paul helps us to understand the "almost" part in 1 Cor 15:17–20: "If Christ has not been raised, your faith is futile and you are still in your sins . . . But in fact Christ has been raised from the dead . . ." The most intimidating giant ever known to man, death itself, would have won, had not there been something after the "it is finished"—the resurrection. The "it is finished' part meant that the price had been paid for Adam's tragic loss to the serpent in Gen 3. What was lost and spoken of in Gen 3:15 was now taken care of and made right. A thousand years before Christ, a giant's head was cut off by David in the Valley of Elah and displayed for all to see. At Golgotha, the Son of David, Christ himself, crushed, decapitated, and displayed the lifeless body of the ultimate serpent. Death's head was splattered on Golgotha that day.

CRUSH IT

C–Call on the Name of the Lord

Christian confidence through and in the face of death is the full awareness of one's end, not the ignorance of it. I won't tell you not to think of death, because I think it can do great good to think of it. Rather, when you think of death, think of it in light of Christ's words: "I am the resurrection and the life." (John 11:25). If you ever feel worried about your own death, or if you are processing the loss of a loved one, hold firmly to this verse.

R–Recall What He Has Done for You

Think of both the cross and the empty tomb. Our Savior proved that he is victorious through his resurrection. We have won through him! Think of the incredible joy that was present the day Jesus rose from the dead. Think of the joy that you will have when you stand before him as he defeats death through you. No weapon or tragedy can ever separate you from his life!

U–Unleash the Authority of Heaven against the Serpent

Whenever you feel fear or worry about death, read John 11:25:

> *I am the resurrection and the life.*

Read this verse as a reminder of the victory found in Jesus. Death has lost its sting. Although we will experience pain and loss in this life, death does not have the final say. Jesus is our resurrection and life. We may not know what eternity will totally be like, but we do undoubtedly know that in Jesus it is good—very good. Meditate on this verse and remind yourself of the peace found in Christ.

S–Stand

Remember the Charles Spurgeon quote at the beginning of this chapter?

> He who learns to die daily while he lives will find it no difficulty to breathe out his soul for the last time.

The best way to crush the serpent of death is to daily live life to the fullest in, through, and for Jesus. Practically, this means living with intentionality. Make it a habit to invite the Holy Spirit to direct your schedule. Look for him and his work as you go about your days. Be purposeful and encouraging with your words, generous with your time and resources and present in the moment. Don't waste your days on meaningless things that don't reflect God's kingdom.

H–Hold the Line

Surround yourself with believers who model the intentionality listed above. Be that type of Christian to others. Encourage one another as you see the day of Christ approaching. Talk about death with others and reflect with them on the victory in Christ and the importance of living well today. Make meeting with another believer or group a normal part of your schedule, whether that is once a week, every other week, or once a month.

IT–Death

The greatest weapon of the serpent has become the greatest joy for the Christian. Just like Jesus, the cross is transformed from a symbol of terror to a symbol of hope. Death is now the means by which we stand perfect before the throne of God, and we will live with him forever and ever.

10

Serpent Crushing, Giant Slaying Rhythm

"Crush: to press something very hard so that it is broken or its shape is destroyed."—Cambridge Dictionary[1]

In the end, it's all about the beginning. How will you start in your efforts to be a serpent crusher? May I make a suggestion? You have to have a rhythm. That's what all of the human serpent crushers became adept at, and that is what Jesus was perfect at. You must begin by asking Jesus to take over your life and pull you into the vortex that is the life of the second Adam, the seed of the woman. This is an entirely new existence. I have no doubt that it will be marked by good times and ones that don't feel so good; but as the apostle Paul reminds us, your life is now hidden with Christ in God (see Col 3:3). This means that the serpent can't reach you there. You are free to hide from him in Jesus and be coached up, protected, empowered, and released to slay serpents on his behalf. Serpent crushers live out of a serpent-crushing rhythm.

First, the power of this rhythm is not found in you. Jesus said himself that you didn't have to do it on your own. He sent a helper. His Spirit came at Pentecost to us all (see Acts 2:1–41). To all who are in him, there is the help from heaven to live in the

1. "Crush."

kingdom rhythm. Ask him for his help, and it is always there. Christ lives through us because he lives in us. This is foundational, and you will not be able to crush the serpents in your life if you do not understand that Jesus lives in you and through you. He is there to help you live as the serpent crusher that you were intended to be. Be encouraged by his words:

> 16 And I will ask the Father, and he will give you another Advocate, to be with you forever. 17 This is the Spirit of truth, whom the world cannot receive, because it neither sees him nor knows him. You know him, because he abides with you, and he will be in you. (John 14:16–17)

Second, this rhythm is not a one-time event. It is a day in, day out process that is completed when we stand before the Father. This book is meant to be a resource to refer to, not a one time read front to back. Each area will need to be returned to again and again, and done so with other believers. Like an axe that is used daily, we need to be continually sharpened in God's presence.

Third, this rhythm is meant to be done in community. That is why we included the "Hold the Line" section in each chapter. The Christian life is meant to be done in community, and serpents are crushed much easier when there are several feet stepping on them repeatedly. Don't think that you're special and that you can figure this out by yourself. You can't. Don't be a knucklehead.

We've included a summary of the *crush its* from the book in this final chapter. When you return to this content, use this list as a brief guide to help you continue to crush every serpent in your life. Let's review Jesus' personal rhythm displayed through the Bible and how he lived and crushed the serpent in every area and every aspect of his life. I have no doubt that if you take the encouragement and tactics presented in this little book, you will engage in the life of a serpent crusher. You will no doubt be successful. I also have no doubt that you will be assaulted. You will be struck at by the old viper himself. But, take heart, the great serpent crusher lives in you, on you, and shouts through you that *it is finished*! The serpent who crushed the original Adam has been rendered eternally powerless. While he has some tactics that are temporary and somewhat effective, his time is limited, and his cause is lost. For the great serpent crusher forever shouts victory through you and those like you. Those who dare to stop being crushed and become the crushers themselves. Yes, you will be involved in renaming places that have been stolen by the serpent and his seed, because the giants live there no more. Renaming them in the name of the one who was, is, and ever shall be the seed of the woman . . . the seed of a serpent-crushing generation.

Now, let's go and crush some serpents like Jesus did!

Jesus Crushed His Time

Mark 1:35

> *In the morning, while it was still very dark, he got up and*
> *went out to a deserted place, and there he prayed.*

His days were spent focused upon getting to the cross and crushing the giant serpent of death. As he did this, he spoke to as many people as he could. The religious were mostly offended. Harlots were cleansed. Lepers were healed. The blind saw. Hungry people were fed—and the list goes on and on. God and people, people and God. Relationships, relationships, and more relationships. Crush your time by spending it on the right things. In order to crush your time like he did, you should . . .

C–Call on the Name of the Lord

Take a breath. Regularly pause at the beginning of the day (and in the middle of it) to turn your eyes towards Jesus. Look beyond immediate concerns and responsibilities, towards Christ. Breathe deeply as you pause in his presence. Thank him for your breath. Thank him for your life. Thank him for your time.

R–Recall What He Has Done for You

Remember all of the hectic, crazy things that God has walked with you through, especially if you feel overwhelmed right now. Remember his faithfulness and thank him for it.

U–Unleash the Authority of Heaven against the Serpent

Turn these first two steps into a prayer. Speak directly to your thoughts of hurry, urgency, panic, and worry. Speak with God slowly, surrendering your schedule and thoughts to him. Meditate and repeat specific scripture verses that teach this principle. Psalm 63 is a passage that will be of much help to you if you are feeling overwhelmed. . .

1 O God, you are my God, I seek you,
my soul thirsts for you;
my flesh faints for you,
as in a dry and weary land where there is no water.
2 So I have looked upon you in the sanctuary,
beholding your power and glory.
3 Because your steadfast love is better than life,
my lips will praise you.
4 So I will bless you as long as I live;
I will lift up my hands and call on your name.
5 My soul is satisfied as with a rich feast,
and my mouth praises you with joyful lips
6 when I think of you on my bed,
and meditate on you in the watches of the night;
7 for you have been my help,
and in the shadow of your wings I sing for joy.
8 My soul clings to you;
your right hand upholds me.
9 But those who seek to destroy my life
shall go down into the depths of the earth;

> *10 they shall be given over to the power of the sword,*
> *they shall be prey for jackals.*
> *11 But the king shall rejoice in God;*
> *all who swear by him shall exult,*
> *for the mouths of liars will be stopped.*

S–Stand

Choose your schedule early in the day. Incorporate a planner or calendar into this process. Designate specific times for work, relaxation, family, outreach, and, most importantly, time with Jesus. A regular rhythm like this will help you reflect your serpent-crushing King's priorities.

H–Hold the Line

Plan at least one time each week to meet or talk with another believer about what it means to crush your time like Jesus. Maybe find someone who you know crushes this area, and ask them about their own personal rhythm.

IT–Your Time

The serpent would like to see you unengaged and lazy, or, on the other hand, so busy that you become burned out. The rhythm of Jesus the serpent crusher leads towards peace and purpose, expressed in an effective life. Let's *crush our time* like Jesus did.

Jesus Crushed His Health

Luke 9:23

> *Then he said to them all, 'If any want to become my followers, let them deny themselves and take up their cross daily and follow me.*

Gal 2:19b–20

> *I have been crucified with Christ; 20 and it is no longer I who live, but it is Christ who lives in me. And the life I now live in the flesh I live by faith in the Son of God, who loved me and gave himself for me.*

1 Cor 6:19

> *Or do you not know that your body is a temple of the Holy Spirit within you, which you have from God, and that you are not your own?*

Jesus carried a physical cross and died on a hill. He commanded his disciples, and all of us, to take up our own crosses and follow him. We must walk in the power of his finished, serpent-crushing work and die to ourselves daily—this includes our physicality. Our diets, exercise habits, and any physical coping mechanisms are all to be nailed to the cross with Jesus. Your body is a temple of his Spirit, and Jesus deserves the proper reverence and discipline in it. In order to crush your health like he did, you should . . .

C–Call on the Name of the Lord

Take a step back from your daily routine. Ask Jesus to show you if you are using anything to cope with life. Do you rely unhealthily upon food? Do you spend too much time on a screen? Do you spend too much time working? Ask Jesus about these issues in prayer. Surrender your habits to him. It may be that some of these areas need to be crushed. Have they become giants that intimidate and/or control you?

R–Recall What He Has Done for You

Spend some time remembering moments or seasons in your life when you had victory and success in the area of your health. This could include physical, emotional, or spiritual health. If you are having trouble thinking of anything, and feel like you are getting crushed, imagine what it would be like if you, through Jesus, became the crusher. Imagine the time, energy, and purpose that will be yours when you reverse this situation.

U–Unleash the Authority of Heaven against the Serpent

Read Luke 2:52 out loud:

> *And Jesus increased in wisdom and in stature, and in divine and human favor.*

This verse speaks of how Jesus grew. You are called to follow and imitate him. Ask Jesus to lead and guide you to live with the same excellence and discipline that he did. Ask him to crush these things through you. Write down this verse and put it somewhere so that you will see it and remind yourself of what Jesus will crush through you as it relates to your health.

S–Stand

Prayerfully write down areas of your life where you feel you are being crushed. Some examples might be:

- Physical health
- Mental/emotional health
- Spiritual health
- Relational health

After writing this list, think about one tangible step you might take this week in each area. Steps could include a workout this week, journaling in a notebook, researching potential pastoral counselors or therapists, or starting a new Bible reading plan. This type of intentionality is a great start to seeing lasting change and reversing the roles of who is getting crushed and who is doing the crushing.

H–Hold the Line

> "For a habit to stay changed, people must believe that change is possible. And most often, that belief only emerges with the help of a group."[2]

See if you might find a person or a group of people who are submitted to the serpent crusher, and who will encourage and keep you accountable in these areas. Lasting change is much more likely to occur when you practice healthy serpent crushing with fellow serpent crushers.

IT–Your Health

God is interested in every facet of your being and calls you to live in freedom. The serpent will take any opportunity to erode your health through compromises and yielding to temptation. Stay strong and remember that. . .

1 Cor 6:19

> . . .*your body is a temple of the Holy Spirit within you, which you have from God, and that you are not your own?*

Jesus Crushed His Words

Jesus spoke the word. He was also referred to by his best friend on this earth, the apostle John, as the Word. Jesus was the Word, and he spoke the Word. A powerful and reverberating kingdom effect. "The Word" in John 1 doesn't only mean the verbal word, but so much more. It means the actual strategy or logic of heaven. Jesus is heaven's tactical response to the serpent. Speak Jesus, think Jesus, act Jesus, and serpents get crushed. We must speak the truth of Christ's message to every person and every serpent. In order to crush your words like Jesus did, you must know what

2. Duhigg, *Power of Habit*, 92.

the Word says about the awesome power of that Word when it is reflected in and lived through your life. . .

> *1 In the beginning was the Word, and the Word was with God, and the Word was God. 2 he was in the beginning with God. 3 All things came into being through him, and without him not one thing came into being. What has come into being 4 in him was life, and the life was the light of all people. 5 The light shines in the darkness, and the darkness did not overcome it. (John 1:1–5)*

C–Call on the Name of the Lord

Before or during your conversations, take a mental pause. It might be just for a second, but take that moment to invite Jesus, the serpent crusher, into that conversation. Ask him to guide your words and to be the lens through which you receive words from others.

R–Recall What He Has Done for You

Recall the effect that the words of others have had on you. Think specifically about an encouraging word or two that bolstered your faith. Reflect on the power of those words in your life.

U–Unleash the Authority of Heaven against the Serpent

Speak encouragement to others. Seek to build others up in the truth because of Christ's serpent-crushing presence in you. When others speak negatively towards you, remember Christ's truth about you and lean on this verse. Write it on a notecard or on your phone. Have it in a place where you will regularly see it, reflect on it, and be empowered by God's serpent-crushing Spirit to live it:

Eph 4:29

29 Let no evil talk come out of your mouths, but only what is useful for building up, as there is need, so that your words may give grace to those who hear.

S–Stand

Intentionally seek to grow in your words. Set a reminder to send an encouraging word to someone regularly. If you are married, leave an affectionate note for your wife and compliment something specific about her. Give a friend a call just to simply encourage and pray for them. Greet the quiet neighbor or coworker who is difficult to approach.

H–Hold the Line

Surround yourself with people who crush their words through Jesus. If you do not have one yet, prayerfully seek a mentor who will speak encouragement into your life. Do your part to create a serpent-crushing encouraging culture in the lives of those around you.

IT–Your Mouth

The New Testament describes Jesus as "the Word." God has charged all communication with the power for great good or for great evil. When you surrender your words to Jesus, you follow him in revealing God's life to yourself and to the world.

Jesus Crushed It in His Mind

Jesus experienced thoughts and emotions and he lived with them. He cried, he got angry, he felt alone. In Gethsemane, he was so emotionally charged that he even sweated drops of blood. But he never, ever sinned in the midst of these serpent-induced attacks.

Yes, he was assaulted and crushed. He was beaten and ripped to the point of spilling his blood; however, as we have repeatedly stated—it was all planned. He came, according to the Gen 3:15 proclamation that prophesied it would happen. That was not the end of the story. We know that after the terrible crushing, he in fact crushed everything that crushed him. The python-like death grip that sent him to a grave and endeavors to grip and cause fear in every son of Adam was crushed. The resurrection of this second Adam, was, is and forever will be a crushing defeat to the serpent. The resurrected seed of the woman is now the head of a whole new race of superhumans—ones who can submit not only their physical bodies to Jesus, but their emotions as well. Sadness, joy, depressions, anxieties, and every other feeling, both positive and negative, under the sun are to be given to him. In order to crush your emotions like Jesus did, you must . . .

C–Call on the Name of the Lord

When you are struggling with your thoughts, perception of self, perception of others, or emotions, take a breath, then out loud or in your mind speak the name of Jesus. Say it again and again and again. Remember this verse, commit it to memory and be ready to crush the serpents who will try and crush your emotions . . .

Phil 2:9–11

> *9 Therefore God also highly exalted him and gave him the name that is above every name, 10 so that at the name of Jesus every knee should bend, in heaven and on earth and under the earth, 11 and every tongue should confess that Jesus Christ is Lord, to the glory of God the Father.*

R–Recall What He Has Done for You

Reflect on the cross itself. Jesus' sacrifice was the greatest proof of your worth and the worth of others. Focus on the cross in the midst of your challenging thoughts or emotions. Remember this verse, commit it to memory, and be ready to crush serpents with it . . .

Heb 2:14–15

> *14 Since, therefore, the children share flesh and blood, he himself likewise shared the same things, so that through death he might destroy the one who has the power of death, that is, the devil, 15 and free those who all their lives were held in slavery by the fear of death.*

U–Unleash the Authority of Heaven against the Serpent

Constantly fill your mind with Scripture. Write especially powerful verses on a notecard, listen to longer passages in the car, and commit Scripture to memory based on particular difficulties you might be facing. Here are some possible examples:

To crush anger: Luke 23:34

To crush anxiety: Ps 23

To crush laziness: 1 Cor 9:24

To crush worry about finances: Matt 6:25–27

Repeat these verses as prayers throughout the day, whenever your mind is attacked in a specific area.

S–Stand

Eliminate or limit things in your life that hinder or hurt your mental health. These might be excessive amounts of social media, television, work, food, or time spent looking at your finances. Replace these areas with healthy habits such as exercise, reading, journaling, prayer, or a new, healthy hobby.

H–Hold the Line

Discuss the last two points with another believer, such as a mentor, pastor, or fellow Christian who is more mature and has crushed these emotion-crushing serpents in their own life. Make it a regular part of your rhythm to meet with this serpent-crushing mentor for accountability and encouragement.

IT–Your Mind

Your mind. Remember that what you feed grows. What you plant in the soil of your mind grows either into a healthy, strong rooted tree, watered by the living water that flows out of God's word, or a weak, sickly, and dying blade of grass that will wither, fade away, and die. Meditate and think about things that are good, right, healthy, living, new and beautiful . . .

Phil 4:8–9

> *8 Finally, beloved, whatever is true, whatever is honorable, whatever is just, whatever is pure, whatever is pleasing, whatever is commendable, if there is any excellence and if there is anything worthy of praise, think about these things. 9 Keep on doing the things that you have learned and received and heard and seen in me, and the God of peace will be with you.*

Jesus Crushed His Sexuality

Jesus was a man, and he crushed his sexuality. He did not objectify women—this is crucial. He honored the women in his life and never used them selfishly for his own sexual purposes. He cared deeply for his mother, listening to her while he was living, then making sure that she had a place to live even as he was dying a horrible death on the cross. He certainly understood that a healthy portion of one's masculine authority was tied to sexuality and the manner in which a man treated women. He said as much in the following verses . . .

> *20 But I have this against you: you tolerate that woman Jezebel, who calls herself a prophet and is teaching and beguiling my servants to practice fornication and to eat food sacrificed to idols. 21 I gave her time to repent, but she refuses to repent of her fornication. 22 Beware, I am throwing her on a bed, and those who commit adultery with her I am throwing into great distress, unless they repent of her doings; 23 and I will strike her children dead. And all the churches will know that I am the one who searches minds and hearts, and I will give to each of you as your works deserve. 24 But to the rest of you in Thyatira, who do not hold this teaching, who have not learned what some call "the deep things of Satan", to you I say, I do not lay on you any other burden; 25 only hold fast to what you have until I come. 26 To everyone who conquers and continues to do my works to the end,*
>
> *I will give authority over the nations;*
>
> *27 to rule them with an iron rod,*
>
> *as when clay pots are shattered—*
>
> *28 even as I also received authority from my Father. To the one who conquers I will also give the morning star. 29 Let anyone who has an ear listen to what the Spirit is saying to the churches.* (Rev 2:20–29)

Let's be serpent-crushing conquerors!

C–Call on the Name of the Lord

When your thoughts and heart rate begin to speed up in the presence of sexual temptation, slow yourself down. If possible, remove yourself from a compromising situation by going outdoors or somewhere public. Speak the name of Jesus over your mind and your physical desires.

R–Recall What He Has Done for You

If you are married, remind yourself of your spouse and the gift that they are to you. Look at a picture of her. Think back to the pure joy it is to be in God's presence without guilt or shame. Reflect on the honor that it is to be God's child and the sacrifice Jesus made for you to be clean.

U–Unleash the Authority of Heaven against the Serpent

Choose a Scripture to be your battle verse. Whenever tempting thoughts come to mind, repeat that Scripture several times. Here are some examples of verses you could commit to memory for this purpose:

- 2 Timothy 2:22
- 1 Thessalonians 4:3–8
- 1 Corinthians 10:13
- 2 Corinthians 10:3–4
- Ephesians 5:11–14

S–Stand

Identify your areas of weakness and make a plan to fight temptation in that area. If you struggle with sexual temptation on the internet, look into accountability software such as Covenant Eyes. Throw out every pornographic magazine, video, or picture you have in your house. Delete any hookup apps you have used for sexual experiences. Identify the most common times, places, and situations in which you fail sexually through masturbation. Write down a specific plan on how you will flee temptation when it arises. For example, you could:

1. Remove yourself from the tempting situation by going on a run, meeting up with a friend, or at least going to a different room.

2. Repeat your memory verse out loud or in your mind.

3. Engage in physical activity like push ups, sit ups, etc. to burn some energy.

4. Reach out to someone you are honest with and be accountable via a call or text.

H–Hold the Line

Community is incredibly important in regards to sexual purity. You can't do this alone. Find a serpent-crushing friend who you know has experienced victory in this area themselves and ask them about their strategy. Share your thoughts from the last point and ask them to be your accountability partner in the areas in which you struggle.

IT–Your Sexuality

The serpent wants to see the gift of sexuality perverted from its original intent. This area can be one of the greatest gifts or greatest weaknesses in life. When submitted to God, your sexuality worships the Father and proclaims the beauty and wholeness of his kingdom. Let's crush it like Jesus did!

Jesus Crushed His Heritage

Jesus crushed his, yours, mine and every other son of the first Adam's heritage. He came to take back what the serpent stole. The slithery one was living in Jesus' house. The heritage of mankind had been stolen and Jesus charged the hill like Caleb and took it back. He went into the pit with a lion and made it safe again. He established himself on the top of Golgotha, then brought the crowning glory when he got up on the third day. He took his heritage back, so you could take yours. No history, trend, or generational curse in our lives can overcome the victorious power of Jesus Christ.

C–Call on the Name of the Lord

Whenever you start to believe that your identity or actions are more influenced by your family than by Jesus, repeat this prayer in your mind or out loud: "Jesus, I need your help to redeem my heritage." Repeat this prayer five, ten, twenty times.

R–Recall What He Has Done for You

The greatest proof that you are a new creation is the cross. Think about the payment Jesus made for you and how that payment supercedes any other curse, habit, or identity. Who are you in him? What has he brought you out of? Who do you want to be in him?

It may help to write your thoughts down from this section and keep that note as an encouragement for yourself in the future. When you struggle in this area, read the note again.

U–Unleash the Authority of Heaven against the Serpent

Read 2 Cor 5:17 over your life:

> *So if anyone is in Christ, there is a new creation: everything old has passed away; see, everything has become new!*

Write this verse down, and put it where you will see it every day. Read it slowly, thinking about each word. Commit it to memory. Remind others that their newness in Jesus is greater than any physical or family tie.

S–Stand

Identify the voices that you are listening to. Are there people in your life that constantly remind you of who you used to be, or who your family is? Are there those who put you down when you have the courage to dream? Has isolation led to your thoughts spiraling? Identify the times and situations that lead you to accepting thoughts of a heritage that isn't from Jesus. Ask God how you can limit these interactions—then *stand*!

H–Hold the Line

Share the previous points with another believer or group. Invite brothers and sisters into this process of walking in Christ's new life. As stated above, prioritize encouraging others in their struggles.

IT–Your Heritage

Legacies can be a very powerful or a very destructive thing. The momentum of good and bad decisions reverberates generationally. Through the life of Christ, you are called and equipped to crush every curse and lay a foundation of faithfulness for those who will come after you.

Jesus Crushed Death

Jesus crushed the serpent of death. The apostle Paul says that if he didn't we are a "pitiful people" (1 Cor 15:19). This means that if Jesus didn't rise physically from the dead, that we are wasting our time—but we know that he did rise. And while the head of the serpent was in fact crushed on Golgotha when he proclaimed, "*it is finished*," the serpent was eternally decapitated when Jesus resurrected on the third day. In Gen 3:15, God mentioned that the serpent would strike at Jesus' heel. But as he struck at Jesus' heel, the cross crushed his head, and the resurrection would ultimately finish the job. Now, it is your job to sit in that fact, walk in that fact, and stand in the midst of a culture that is often serpent-like. We sit with Christ at the right hand of the Father. We walk in that authority each day and we stand in faith concerning those facts. We can have hope and peace in the face of death and are called to bring that hope and peace to others.

C–Call on the Name of the Lord

Christian confidence in death is the full awareness of one's end, not the ignorance of it. I won't tell you not to think of death, because I think it can do you a great good to think of it. I want to challenge you to think of it in light of Christ's words: "I am the resurrection and the life" (John 11:25). If you ever feel worried about your own death or if you are processing the loss of a loved one, hold firmly to this verse.

R–Recall What He Has Done for You

Think of both the cross and the empty tomb. Your Savior proved that he is victorious through his resurrection. You have serpent-crushing victory through him! Think of the incredible joy that was present the day Jesus rose from the dead. Think of the joy that you will have when you stand before him as he defeats death through you. No weapon or tragedy can ever separate you from his life!

U–Unleash the Authority of Heaven against the Serpent

Whenever you feel fear or worry about death, read John 11:25:

> *I am the resurrection and the life.*

Read this verse as a reminder of the victory found in Jesus. Death has lost its sting. Although we will experience pain and loss in this life, death does not have the final word. Jesus is your resurrection and life. You may not know what eternity will be like exactly, but you do know that in Jesus, it is good—very good. Meditate on this verse and remind yourself of the peace found in Christ.

S–Stand

> "He who learns to die daily while he lives will find it no difficulty to breathe out his soul for the last time."
> —Charles Spurgeon

The best way to crush the serpent of death is to live life to the fullest each day—in Jesus. Practically, this means living with intentionality. Make it a habit to invite the Holy Spirit to direct your schedule. Look for him and his work as you go about your day. Be purposeful and encouraging with your words, generous with your time and resources, and present in the moment. Don't waste your days on meaningless things that don't reflect God's kingdom.

H–Hold the Line

Surround yourself with serpent-crushing believers who model the intentionality listed above. Be that type of Jesus follower to others. Encourage one another. Talk about death with others and reflect with them on the victory of Christ, the serpent crusher. Talk about living well today. Make a decision to meet with another believer or group to talk about these things, whether that is once a week, every other week, or once a month.

IT–Death

The greatest weapon of the serpent has become the greatest joy for the Jesus follower. Just like Jesus, the cross is transformed from a symbol of terror to a symbol of hope. Death is now the means by which we stand before the throne of God, and we will live with him forever and ever, having eternally crushed the serpent of death.

Bibliography

"10 Spurgeon Quotes on Dying Well." The Spurgeon Center. https://www.spurgeon.org/resource-library/blog-entries/10-spurgeon-quotes-on-dying-well.

"15 Stunning Statistics About Porn in the Church." Sep 19, 2018. https://www.trunews.com/stream/15-stunning-statistics-about-porn-in-the-church.

Adamson, Andrew, dir. *The Chronicles of Narnia: The Lion, the Witch, and the Wardrobe.* 2005; Burbank, CA: Buena Vista Pictures Distribution.

Adeleke, Remi. "Every Hero Has A Villain." Sermon. Tulsa, OK. Sep 2019.

"Adult Obesity Facts." CDC. https://www.cdc.gov/obesity/data/adult.html.

Atkins, Rodney. "Watching You." *If You're Going Through Hell*, Curb Records, 2006.

Avildsen, John G., dir. *Rocky.* 1976; Hollywood, CA: United Artists.

Besemer, Sytske, et al. "A Systematic Review and Meta-Analysis of the Intergenerational Transmission of Criminal Behavior." *Aggression and Violent Behavior* 37 (2017) 161–78.

"Better." Cambridge Dictionary. https://dictionary.cambridge.org/us/dictionary/english/better

Brenner, Grant Hilary. "My Partner's Parents Cheated. Will My Partner Cheat on Me?" Psychology Today. https://www.psychologytoday.com/us/blog/experimentations/201712/my-partners-parents-cheated-will-my-partner-cheat-on-me.

Brody, Debra and Qiuping Gu. "Antidepressant Use Among Adults: United States, 2015-2018." CDC. https://www.cdc.gov/nchs/products/databriefs/db377.htm.

Chapman, Harry. "Cat's in the Cradle." *Verities & Balderdash*, Elektra, 1974.

"Crush." Cambridge Dictionary. https://dictionary.cambridge.org/us/dictionary/english/crush.

"Drug Abuse Statistics." https://drugabusestatistics.org/

Duhigg, Charles. *The Power of Habit.* New York, NY: Random House, 2014.

Hamilton, James. "The Skull Crushing Seed of the Woman: Inner-Biblical Interpretation of Genesis 3:15." *Southern Baptist Journal of Theology* 10 (2006) 30-54. https://jimhamilton.info/wp-content/uploads/2008/04/hamilton_sbjt_10-2.pdf.

Hansel, Tim. *When I Relax I Feel Guilty.* Elgin, IL: Chariot Family, 1979.

"Heritage." Merriam-Webster. https://www.merriam-webster.com/dictionary/heritage.

"Herod Antipas." Britannica. https://www.britannica.com/biography/Herod-Antipas.

Hummel, Charles. *Tyranny of the Urgent.* Downers Grove: InterVarsity, 1994.

"Internet Pornography by the Numbers." Webroot. https://www.webroot.com/us/en/resources/tips-articles/internet-pornography-by-the-numbers#:~:text=40%20million%20American%20people%20regularly,of%20porn%20viewers%20are%20women.

Jackson, Peter, dir. *Lord of the Rings: Return of the King.* 2003; Burbank, CA: New Line Cinema.

Janson, Chris. "Drunk Girl." *Everybody,* Warner Bros., 2017.

Kasdan, Lawrence, dir. *Silverado.* 1985; Culver City, CA: Columbia Pictures.

Lewis, C. S. *Letters of C. S Lewis.* New York: Harcourt Brace Jovanovich, 1966.

———. *The Horse and His Boy.* New York: HarperCollins, 1994.

Lucas, George, dir. *Star Wars: Return of the Jedi.* 1983; Los Angeles: 20th Century Fox.

MacDonald, George. "A Meditation on Becoming a Self." In *Selected Readigs from C. S. Lewis, George MacDonald: An Anthology.* New York: MacMillan, 1947.

Marshall, Taylor. "Golgotha: The Word Symbolizes a Beautiful Reality!" Taylor Marshall, Mar 28, 2013. https://taylormarshall.com/2013/03/golgotha-word-symbolizes-beautiful.html.

Miller, Jessica. "Sleep Medication Addiction Statistics." https://www.addictionguide.com/sleeping-pills/statistics/.

Minkove, Judy F. "New Research and Insights into Substance Use Disorder." https://www.hopkinsmedicine.org/news/articles/new-research-and-insights-into-substance-use-disorder.

Murray, Lorraine. "Kim Jong-Un." https://www.britannica.com/biography/Kim-Jong-Eun.

"National Office for Suicide Prevention Annual Report – 2021." National Office for Suicide Prevention (Ireland). https://www.hse.ie/eng/services/list/4/mental-health-services/connecting-for-life/publications/nosp-annual-report-2021.pdf.

Nee, Watchman. *Journeying Towards the Spiritual.* Richmond, VA: Christian Fellowship, 2006.

Perowne, Stewart Henry. "Herod, King of Judaea." Britannica. https://www.britannica.com/biography/Herod-king-of-Judaea.

Peterson, Eugene. *The Contemplative Pastor*. Grand Rapids: Eerdmans, 1989.

"Revelation 2 – Jesus' Letters to the Churches." https://enduringword.com/bible-commentary/revelation-2/.

"Saddam Hussein." Britannica. https://www.britannica.com/biography/Saddam-Hussein.

Steigerwald, Bill. "Lofty Ideals." *Pittsburgh Post-Gazette*, Nov 9, 1998.

Shenk, Rick. "David and Goliath—Think Again!" Bethlehem College and Seminary. https://bcsmn.edu/david-and-goliath/.

Simeon, Charles. "Discourse 7: The Seed of the Woman." Biblia Plus, n.d. https://www.bibliaplus.org/en/commentaries/168/cjarles-simeon-horae-homileticae/genesis/3/15.

Thomas, Gary. *Sacred Marriage*. Grand Rapids: Zondervan, 2015.

Thoreau, Henry David. *Walden and On the Duty of Civil Disobedience*. Minneapolis: First Avenue Editions, 2014.

Tift, J. Neil. "A Father's Place: The Importance of Male Involvement in Early Childhood Development." https://www.continued.com/early-childhood-education/articles/father-s-place-importance-male-23357.

"US Leads Overall Spend in $828 Billion Physical Activity Market." Global Wellness Institute. https://globalwellnessinstitute.org/press-room/press-releases/us-leads-overall-spend-in-828-billion-physical-activity-market/.

Voth, Jeff. *Cavetime: God's Plan for Man's Escape from Life's Assaults*. Redding, CA: Printopya, 2021.

Voth, Jeff and Joshua Beck. *Jesus is the Thesis*. Eugene, OR: Wipf and Stock, 2022.

Williamson, Celia. "These are the Customers Who Support Sex-trafficking in the US." The Conversation, Aug 29, 2019. https://theconversation.com/these-are-the-customers-who-support-sex-trafficking-in-the-us-121866.